A VINTAGE PORT

A VINTAGE PORT

LARNE AND ITS PEOPLE

Alf McCreary

GREYSTONE 2000

First published in the United Kingdom, 2000
by Greystone Press,
Antrim, Northern Ireland

ISBN 1 870157 29 X

Illustrations used on title page and at the start of each chapter
are Code Flags denoting "A Vintage Port".

Designed by Rodney Miller Associates, Belfast
Printed in Northern Ireland by W&G Baird Ltd., Antrim

FOREWORD

The story of the Port of Larne stretches from the mists of time in the Middle Stone Age, through the pre-Christian centuries and the Viking raids, to the more modern history of the 19th and 20th centuries, and the development of the most modern facilities and technologies which have made Larne a major channel for commercal and passenger traffic in these islands.

It is a story of vision, ingenuity and hard work which turned a small harbour into a thriving Port. Larne developed significantly from the mid-19th century, and particularly after the Second World War when the world-wide revolution in unitised traffic and the increased mobility of tourists and other travellers necessitated far-reaching technological and other major changes.

There were years of immense difficulty, including two World Wars, periods of economic depression, and times of tragic loss as in the Princess Victoria disaster. But throughout all these challenges, changes and setbacks, the people showed remarkable resilience, a determination to learn from the past and to look to the future, and a resolve to make Larne an outstanding modern Port.

They did so with their own style and brand of humour. The history of Larne is the story of major characters like James Chaine, who did most to establish the Port in the 19th century, and also of Colonel Frank Bustard who in the mid-twentieth century had the vision of a new system of moving goods in bulk, and who helped to make Larne a most profitable part of the container revolution.

It is also the story of countless ordinary people who did their day's work at the Port and made their own mark on the passage of time. There were also many seafarers whose knowledge of winds and weathers and whose skill and sometimes great bravery helped to pilot vessels to safe harbour through stormy seas. Many of these sailors led colourful lives , which themselves could fill a book, and between these lines you will discover more than a whiff of the daring, adventure and even romance of life on the high seas.

The history of the Port of Larne is also the story of thousands of Ulster emigrants who left to start a new life in America, or in other parts of the United Kingdom, or further afield, and although it is a story of commercial and technological success, it is at heart the human story of so many people whose lives were shaped, or touched in passing, by what happened at the Port.

For me it has been an adventure to research and to write this story, and a privilege to be able to share with so many people who talked to me so freely. And as we record our own history by embarking on a new Millennium, we should also pay tribute to all those - past and present - who helped to make the Port of Larne what it is today.

Alf McCreary,
6 April 2000.

ACKNOWLEDGEMENTS

The author wishes to acknowledge the help of many people who made this publication possible. They include Denis Galway, Director and General Manager of Larne Harbour Ltd. and all his staff for their considerable help and kindness; my wife Hilary for her support; Pauline Allen for helping to prepare the manuscript; Ivan Ewart for photography; Jim McCarlie and Captain William Close for their background information; Stephen Ranson, P&O Group Information Manager, for helpful suggestions on certain parts of the text; Ann McIlrath and Ian Duffin for their help with some early material; Heather Stanley of the Public Record Office of Northern Ireland, Pat McClean of the Ulster Museum, Kenneth Anderson of the Ulster Folk and Transport Museum, Grianne MacLochlainn of the National Library of Ireland, and Len Tweedie, Promotions Manager of the Belfast Telegraph, for their help with illustrations; Mrs Margaret McIlrath for permission to quote part of the material from her late husband's work; Miss Isabelle Logan for the reminiscences and material about her father; Mrs Jane Ludlow for permission to quote from her Dissertation for Queen's University; Tommy Shields for a stirring war-time story and photographs; Tommy Thompson for providing access to relevant material from his library, and all those who so freely gave of their time to help with my research.

The author and publisher would also like to thank the following for the use of material from their publications-the Editors of the Belfast Telegraph, the East Antrim Times, the Larne Times, the Sunday Times, Miles Cowsill and his colleagues, Fraser G. MacHaffie, and all others whose scholarly and literary sources are quoted, and duly acknowledged in the text.

In particular, the author and publisher would like to thank Bryan McCabe of W&G Baird Limited, the printers, and Arnold Gormley and John Hamill of Rodney Miller Associates, the designers, for their skill and assistance in the production and presentation of this volume.

CONTENTS

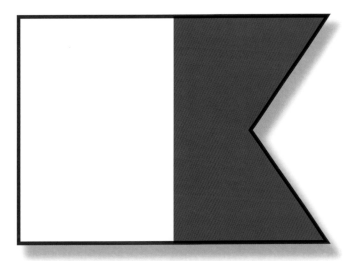

CHAPTER 1

FROM THE MISTS

"We came very suddenly upon Larne, and at the same moment that we turned over the edge of the deep glen on which it lies, the sun broke out upon the lovely bay and village below, illuminating the whole scene with a light such as a painter would have chosen. It was, indeed, a delicious picture, and there was something Italian, no less in the soft vapoury light in which it was bathed, than in the position and aspect of the town. Island Magee lay in fine outline across the bay, and on a narrow tongue of land, called the Curraàn, stood the ruins of an old castle, giving a romantic and foreign look to the entire scene. Our car-driver descended too fast for us, though our breakfast was at the foot of the hill, and entering an old-fashioned and narrow street, he deposited us at a small and tidy inn, so like the same thing in Italy, (the street and inn of a small village between Rome and Florence) that the illusion was difficult to shake off."

Watercolour of Larne Harbour c.1825 by Ulster artist Andrew Nicholl.

Courtesy Larne Borough Council

Illusion or not, these are the words used by "NP Willis and J Stirling Coyne Esqrs" who visited the town in 1841 to write a book about the "Scenery and Antiquities of Ireland".[1] Some eight years earlier, a Lieutenant R Boteler described it thus in the Ordnance Survey Memoirs of Ireland: "The town of Larne, called after the parish, is situated at its south end and is the only one in it. It is a market and post town. A very small proportion of it (probably one-tenth) runs into the parish of Inver. It is described as having once carried on a greater export and import trade than at present, for which, from its locality, it seems not unfavourably adapted. It is built close to the Lough called by the same name, but the anchorage for vessels of burden lies at and about Curran Point, being a distance of about three-quarters of a mile to the east, where, from the shelter afforded by Island Magee, they can ride tolerably secure against every stress of weather. The town is well supplied with provisions with the exception of fish, the assortment of which consists in a little sole and grey mullet which are taken in the Lough. It is also well supplied with coal, which is the principal article of fuel owing to the scarcity of turf in the immediate neighbourhood. It forms its chief import trade."[2]

The history of Larne stretches back into the mists of time. In the early 1930's archaeologists from Harvard University uncovered a large quantity of worked flint which had been shaped as knives and other objects along the Curran Point. (This is derived from the Gaelic word "Corran", a hook or sickle which describes well that piece of land jutting into Larne Lough.)

This important archaeological find confirmed that humans had settled here around 3,000 BC in the Mesolithic Period, or Middle Stone Age. This is the term given to the period prior to the Neolithic, or New Stone Age, and is significant because it marks the first evidence of human beings in Ireland. So significant was the discovery that the term "Larnian" was used to describe the whole Mesolithic culture of Ireland, but subsequent excavations at Toome Bay on the shores of Lough Neagh predated the Larne discoveries by some 1,000 years – with the result that the term "Larnian" was later used to describe a flint industry and not a culture.[3]

Larne is believed to have derived its name from Lathar, a son of Hugony the Great, a High King of Ireland in pre-Christian times, who reputedly gave him an area along the Antrim Coast roughly from Glenarm to the River Inver, which became known in the Gaelic as 'Latharna'. It is recorded that the Roman Emperor Serverus around 205 AD described how a Roman galley bound for Scotland was blown off course to a place called "Portus Saxa", which was thought to be Larne Lough. The ancient Greeks also had knowledge of the Antrim Coast, and Ptolemy, the astronomer and geographer of the 2nd Century AD, referred to Islandmagee on one of his maps.

The author Richard Hayward, in his celebrated book "In Praise of Ulster" writes: "Local tradition has it that St Patrick founded a Church at Kilcoan, and there are ancient graveyards in this townland at Kirkland and Whitehouse. And the spot where the Saint crossed Larne Lough in a coracle is still known as St Patrick's Ferry, and the story is told that for this service immunity from accident or danger was bestowed upon the ferryman and his successors for ever."[4]

The raiders from Scandinavia left their mark, and the Lough at one stage was named after a Norse King, called Ulfrich. This became anglicised to Wulfrichfjord and eventually Olderfleet, which is an integral part of modern Larne. Down the centuries, Larne was a seafaring haven which attracted multitudes of sailors and traders, as well as emigrants and indeed immigrants. In the 17th century, regular imports of Scottish coal began arriving at Larne and the number of visitors from Scotland increased. According to one writer "There is little doubt that the progress of Larne as an industrial town was due to its good harbour and its close position – less than 150 minutes sea journey – from mainland Britain."[5] In 1683 Richard Dobbs wrote: "Shipping often stop in this harbour of Olderfleet or Lough Larne, when they are going from Derry and Coleraine to the Southward, and so in their return ... people (with all their goods upon their backs) land here from Scotland . . . every summer without returning."[6]

However, while Larne had an undisputed reputation as a good port, the harbour was not being used to its full potential. In the 18th century there were a number of quays – including a Mr White's at the "near" Bank and a Mr Sweeney's at the "far" Bank – but none in the area of the present harbour. Significantly, there was a lively emigration trade to America from the Town Quay, with one of the earlier ships – The Friend's Goodwill – sailing for Boston in 1717.

In the early 19th century, however, there were important stirrings. In May 1823, a William Agnew obtained a lease for "lives renewable for ever, of the Curran of Larne . . . and the

This engraving illustrates Larne from the top of Millbrae circa 1760-1800. In the foreground is Barkley's Bleachworks, founded in 1750. The isolated building on the Curran Road may have been the old Chapel of Clondumalis, mentioned in Piggot's Directory of Ireland in 1824 as situated on the road to Olderfleet Castle.

Public Record Office of Northern Ireland, PRONI T1129/135

anchorage of the Lough and Curran, Larne, from Lord Donegall." A map of 1832-33 gives the first indication of a quay near the Olderfleet Castle on the eastern side of the Curran. This quay was referred to as the Curran Quay, and was mainly used for the shipment of limestone which was quarried at Waterloo. In 1843, Mr Agnew constructed at a cost of £1,350, a 200 feet long quay, with 16 feet depth of water at low spring tide. This was situated within the present harbour area.[7]

Despite such an initiative, the harbour remained under-used. RH McIlrath in his authoritative "Early Victorian Larne" points out that by 1840 only two Larne ships were engaged in foreign trade – the Chieftain, a vessel of 335 tons, and the Perseverance of 224 tons, both of which worked on the North Atlantic route. The Chieftain, for example, arrived at Larne from Quebec in July 1839 with a cargo of "timber deals and staves etc" and in December the Perseverance reached Larne from Miramichi, New Brunswick, with a similar cargo.

Most trade using the Harbour was local, conducted by a dozen little Larne boats, as well as many others registered as belonging to Islandmagee and other ports on either side of the

North Channel. Among the Larne owners of small boats in 1840, John Smiley, coal importer, was the most prominent, with the Jane, Ann and Squid, of 56, 47 and 43 tons respectively. All these boats relied on wind and sail, but the age of the steam boat had just begun. The News Letter advertised in October 1838 that the "Portrush Steam Navigation Company's Splendid and Powerful Steam Vessel Coleraine would sail to and from Liverpool and Portrush once a week with goods and passengers, 'calling at Larne'."[8] The age of steam was unstoppable, and the advent of the railways meant that a regular link between Larne and Stranraer was only a matter of time.

One of the reasons for the under-use of Larne was the fact that the Government had favoured the Donaghadee-Portpatrick link as the official route for the Royal Mail. A regular passenger, mail and livestock trade had been operating on this route since 1662, and in 1695 an Act was passed enabling a weekly post to be carried across the North Channel. The mail was originally carried in privately-owned vessels, which had a Government subsidy, but the Post Office ran its own mail ships from 1790, and daily sailings were introduced. From April 1837, the service was taken over by the Admiralty, and Royal Navy vessels carried mail across the North Channel until 1848, when all mail services reverted to private contract. The regular sailings between Donaghadee and Portpatrick were withdrawn, "for few passengers ever used them because of the high fares, the poor quality of the ships and the comparative inaccessibility of the two ports which then had no rail connections."[9] In 1861 rail connections were finally established, and a new harbour was completed at Donaghadee in the hope that the Post Office might re-open the mail route, but this did not happen.

Meanwhile, the claims of Larne were being pressed by many, including members of a Post Office Inquiry who in 1836 made a strong recommendation in favour of the Loch Ryan – Larne route. Six years later yet another Select Committee strongly backed Loch Ryan – Larne as the mail route, but there was reluctance to change because of the large amount of money which had been spent on Donaghadee and Portpatrick. Captain George Evans, RN, a member of the previous Post Office Inquiry stated bluntly that attempts to build the piers out from the rock face at Portpatrick were "a useless expense, just the same as throwing the money into the sea." In 1845, Captain Evans was again asked to report on Portpatrick and Donaghadee harbours and he concluded, not without a little understandable exasperation, that "Portpatrick is not, nor ever can be made, a safe harbour either to run for, or depart from, in Westerly or South Westerly gales." However, he described Larne as an "excellent port. A lighthouse has been erected on the eastern side of the entrance and there is a quay 200 feet long with jetties projecting on piles, having 16 feet water at low spring."[10]

In the light of such powerful recommendations for Larne, the rivalry with Donaghadee intensified. In May 1860, an Act had been passed to create the Carrickfergus and Larne Railway and to build over fourteen miles of track from the Belfast and Northern Counties Railway at Carrickfergus to Larne. Rival supporters of both Larne and Donaghadee carried on a lively correspondence in the local papers. In the Belfast News Letter of 16 November 1859, "An Old Inhabitant" of Donaghadee wrote that while Belfast and the County Antrim coast were "enveloped in a dense fog all yesterday . . . we had a lovely day and clear sky . . . the almost total freedom from fogs which this place enjoys, constitutes one of the many strong arguments in its favour of being selected as the Irish packet station." On the Larne side, "Scrutator" rehearsed the familiar arguments in his pamphlet entitled "Some considerations in proof of the superiority of the Packet Route via Larne and Stranraer, contrasted with that via Donaghadee and Portpatrick."[11]

On September 11, 1860 the directors of the Carrickfergus and Larne Railway Company organised one of the first of what would now be called "facility trips" to impress local businessmen concerning the claims of Larne. The steamer Giraffe left Donaghadee at 9.20 am "after an excellent breakfast", and proceeded "at full speed, on a direct line for Portpatrick Harbour." According to the Larne Monthly Visitor, which gave a full account, the trip from "pier to pier might be taken as likely to occupy one hour and thirty four minutes." The Giraffe then made for Lough Ryan, and after "lunch and conversation", the vessel was joined by businessmen from Stranraer and district. The vessel then set off for Larne, and dinner was served. "The viands were of an excellent description, the wines of the choicest vintage." Several speeches were made, no doubt long-winded following such a fine dinner, and after a voyage of two hours and one minute, the Giraffe slowed off Larne. The Donaghadee-Portpatrick journey was obviously shorter, but that was not the whole story. As RH McIlrath coolly points out, tongue-in-cheek: "The excursion had shown that Victorian gentlemen knew how to enjoy themselves, but it proved nothing that was not already common knowledge. Everybody knew that it would be quicker to sail from Donaghadee to Portpatrick, on a calm sea, than from Stranraer to Larne, and everybody knew that this advantage was balanced by the greater safety of Larne and Lough Ryan, and by their accessibility at all times to the largest ships. But the day out had been a first-class exercise in public relations."[12]

In the real world, however, work began some three months later on the railway which would eventually lead to "Larne and Lough Ryan becoming the main channel of communication between the two shores."[13] The construction of the line started in December 1860, with Charles Lanyon as engineer. Only eleven or so years earlier the first students and staff had entered The Queen's University of Belfast, which had been established by Queen Victoria in 1845 as one of the three "Queen's Colleges" in Ireland and which had been designed by Lanyon as one of the most beautiful buildings in the country, which it remains to this day.

In May 1861 the workforce on the railway consisted of 700 men and 89 horses, and the numbers were increased significantly in June to 1,385 men and 200 horses. A month later, the totals were further increased to 1,472 and 257 respectively.[14] Even with such a large workforce, there were considerable difficulties. The tunnel at Whitehead was a major engineering feat, and delays were caused by a landslip between the Bank Quay and Glynn, by heavy seas at Whitehead, and by torrential rains in the winter of 1861-62.[15] Happily, however, the railway from Carrickfergus to Larne was opened on 1 October 1862, less than two months after a new paddle-steamer of raised quarter-deck design, the Briton (purchased for £12,000), took over the Stranraer-Larne route.

The News Letter noted that "those who remember the days, not very long gone by, in which passengers were embarked and landed at Stranraer on the backs of men or in carts or wheelbarrows, will appreciate the convenience and comfort of stepping at once from the steamer into the railway train, or vice-versa." The Briton, when she left Stranraer, encountered a strong headwind and arrived at Larne some 50 minutes late but the passengers made history by stepping on to the train and proceeding at express speed to Belfast, a journey which took forty five minutes, a remarkable achievement in those days.

It seemed as if the new service was secure and that Larne's prosperity was guaranteed. "Larne rejoiced. The celebrations had begun on the previous evening, Tuesday 30 September, when the shops closed early in order to 'allow their young men to join in the amusements.' Barrels of tar were set alight, fireworks were let off, and crowds thronged the streets. An unusual item was the effigy of a twelve-foot man, which was 'borne through the crowd, bowing to the processions in every direction.'" The writer in the Monthly Visitor thought that the device was meaningless, but had to admit that "it certainly had a most ludicrous effect, and attracted vast numbers."

When the Briton arrived on Wednesday afternoon it was met by 'flags flying, music playing, and small cannon firing', and by great crowds of people. Trains other than the boat train gave many people their first experience of travelling in carriages running on rails, pulled along by a steam locomotive. The News Letter reporter wrote that "One old woman with an armful of ling, which she had purchased in Larne and was taking home, on having got a ticket procured for her by a male companion, asked, with the utmost simplicity 'Dae' ye ken what ah'm to do wi' this?' The school-children of the town, including those from the Workhouse School, were given a trip round

A view of Larne from 'Ireland Illustrated' (Cochon, 1831) by GN Wright: engraved by TM Baynes.

Public Record Office of Northern Ireland, PRONI T1129/138

the bay, cheering as they went. Altogether, it was a most satisfactory occasion, and, 'notwithstanding the immense pressure, the slightest accident did not occur.'"[16]

All of this augured well for the future of the Larne-Stranraer link, or so it seemed. The Briton provided a daily service, Sundays excepted, with connecting rail links to London and Londonderry on the Scottish and Irish sides respectively. The Belfast-London journey, with a train via Castle Douglas and Dumfries was scheduled to take 17 hours and 40 minutes. Despite the euphoric start, however, the business did not flourish, though the Briton sustained a service with few interruptions during the winter months and into the summer of 1863, even providing an excursion in July to Red Bay on the Antrim Coast!

Sadly, however, the service lost money. In the first three months the route did not flourish, and an attempt to win a mail contract from the Post Office ended in failure. It had an operating deficit of £1,536. Apparently it came as a surprise to some that the service was, initially at least, running at a loss, and by March of the following year one of the directors moved that the service be discontinued. The majority of the Board were more inclined to give the service a longer period to show its potential, and by the end of September 1863 the half-year figures were a great improvement. It was decided to continue the service for the time being.

However, the financial backers were losing patience. "In November, the Belfast and Northern Counties Railway announced that it was withdrawing from its guarantee on 1 January 1864, unless the other partners agreed to join in building a better boat which 'with greater speed and better accommodation might make the run more attractive.' This agreement was not forthcoming and the service was withdrawn from December 31, 1863."[17]

The Briton was sold in January 1864 to the Bristol General Steam Navigation Company and placed on the Bristol-Waterford run. She was later moved to the Wexford service, until she was sold to the Waterford Steamship Company in 1890. Not long afterwards, she was stranded off Wexford and because of her age she was sold for breaking up – a sad end to what had originally been a hopeful career.

It was a sad end, too, for the first real attempt to operate a profitable and regular steamer service from Larne to Lough Ryan. But all was not lost and the establishment of a permanent link, which would eventually secure the future prosperity of Larne, was not far away. Cometh the hour, cometh the man, and that man was James Chaine.

1. "Scenery and Antiquities of Ireland", Published in 1841 by George Virtue, 26 Ivy Lane, London.
2. "Ordnance Survey Memoirs of Ireland: Parishes of County Antrim III", Edited by Angelique Day and Patrick McWilliams, and Published by the Institute of Irish Studies at The Queen's University of Belfast, p123.
3. Dr David Hume, historian and local journalist, in a talk delivered in Larne on 15 March 1995.
4. "In Praise of Ulster" by Richard Hayward, p84, Published by Arthur Barker Ltd, of London in 1938.
5. FM McKillop in The Corran, Summer 1990, p22, Published by Larne and District Folklore Society.
6. "Early Victorian Larne" by RH McIlrath, pp8-9, Published by Braid Books, 1991, with reference to G Hill in "The MacDonnells of Antrim", p381.
7. "Aspects of Economic and Social Change in the Town of Larne During the Period 1850-1900" by Jane M Ludlow BSc, a Dissertation presented to the School of Social Sciences at The Queen's University of Belfast, September 1991, p58.
8. Op.Cit. RH McIlrath, pp21-23.
9. "Irish Passenger Steamship Services Vol I" by DB McNeill, pp83-84, Published by David and Charles, Newton Abbot in 1969.
10. "The Short Sea Route" by Fraser G MacHaffie, p26, Published by T Stephenson & Sons Ltd, Prescot, Merseyside.
11. Op.Cit. RH McIlrath, p24.
12. Ibid, p24.
13. Ibid, p20.
14. "The Northern Counties Railway Volume I" by JRL Currie, p137, Published by David and Charles, Newton Abbot in 1973.
15. Op.Cit. RH McIlrath, p20.
16. Ibid, p25.
17. Op.Cit. Jane M Ludlow, p62.

Chaine Tower

Courtesy of the Northern Ireland Tourist Board

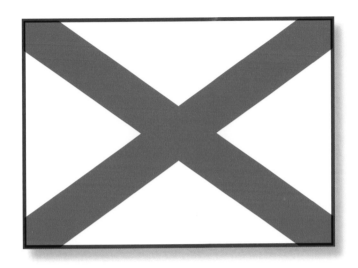

CHAPTER 2

A MAN OF HIS TIME — AND BEYOND

James Chaine, the son of a prosperous Co Antrim linen merchant, purchased the harbour area of Larne in 1866. By Deed Poll dated 28 July, he paid "£9,500 to James Agnew owner and petitioner, in part payment of purchase money of £20,000, and acknowledged debt of £10,500 said to the Court to be due to Charles Agnew for the town and lands of Curran and Drumalis containing 203 acres, 1 rood and 2 perches statute measure."[1] By 10 May 1882, Chaine had paid off the mortgage of £10,500 with a loan from the Commissioners of Public Works, and obtained full title "to the aforesaid property in fee simple."[2]

The Larne of Chaine's day was very different from that of modern times. RH McIlrath in his "Early Victorian Larne" paints a vivid word-picture of the town: "The life of early Victorian man, in Larne, a mere 150 years ago, was often poor and short, and sometimes nasty, but perhaps no more brutish than it is today, and certainly not solitary, except when that solitariness was self-imposed. He lived in filth and was surrounded by beauty, in an environment that was both sordid and splendid. He and his friends and their families lived in houses that were tiny, 'thatched, old-fashioned, narrow-windowed', and highly insanitary. Water closets were a rare luxury (except in the Workhouse!), and even as late as 1905 two in five of Larne's dwellings had no wc. Waste material was not always rendered inoffensive and harmless, and when the newly-elected Commissioners tried in 1858 to clean up the town, they found it necessary to summon many poor people to the Petty Sessions to be punished by the JPs for their failure to dispose of their 'ashheaps'. . . . Yet if he chose to raise his eyes beyond the houses and the streets, the man in Larne could look on the bare tops of the Antrim hills, the glen of the Inver river, the wooded slopes alongside the Bank Road, and the green fields of Islandmagee, all uninterrupted, then, by the harsh modern angularities of buildings fifteen stories high, tall chimneys and electricity pylons."[3]

There were many characters in the Larne of those days. "In July 1862 Billy Mulholland, a local celebrity and violin player, who was 'frequently engaged in dancing classes', died in the Workhouse, and, unusually, the editor of the Monthly Visitor had nothing good to say about the deceased: '[he] . . . spent a life of indifference to serious considerations . . . [he] died, it is hoped, better than he lived'. The best-remembered itinerant music maker was Jemmy Gilgallion, tin-whistler and just one of the many tramps and beggars who crowded into Larne. An unnamed writer described him: '[he] roamed the town and district, playing a tin whistle, clothed in rags, and wearing several hats stuck on top of each other, in which he stored his belongings . . . he did not often need to solicit alms, for his 'tout ensemble', backed by his dangerous looking cudgel, and his evident capacity to wield it, generally caused people gladly to anticipate his wants'. His answers to the census taker in 1861, recorded in the Monthly Visitor, give a picture of this most colourful of Larne's characters. He spent each night wherever he could find shelter; he was unmarried ('I courted a girl . . . but we never came to the scratch'); he had no trade or profession but would not object to being called a traveller, or tourist, or gentleman ('a gintleman, I think it is, because, ye see, I don't work'); he resented being categorised as a beggarman ('I'm no beggar at all, at all . . . I've often receaved what ye may call prisents – subscriptions – like other gintlemen'); he was born in County Meath, and, in 1861, was about seventy years old, since 'my purty mother presented me, a fine promisin' boy . . . to the ould chap seven years before the ruction in Ireland'. Jemmy Gilgallion was an independent spirit in the midst of hard times. No client he for the Workhouse."[4]

Law and order had its own standards, as this graphic account illustrates: "Major crimes were brought to higher courts. In 1862 Ballymena Quarter Sessions heard how, in Kilwaughter, a young woman had tied the hands of her drunk husband and then cut his throat. He survived, but she still got ten years' penal servitude. The most outrageous case of all these years came before the County Antrim Assize Court in 1840. Evidence was given that in 1839 seven men came across a drunk woman, after midnight, on the road outside Larne. She was repeatedly raped and left to die. 'There was a good deal of drinking', one of the men told the court, 'for it was Easter Monday, which is a kind of play day.' One man was charged with murder, but the court may have been influenced by the doctor's remarkable statement that 'struggling I consider violence on the part of the woman', and the accused was found guilty only of 'aggravated assault' and sentenced to two years in the House of Correction in Belfast. At the same court two men were found guilty of stealing a dozen pairs of socks. They were each sentenced to ten years' transportation."[5]

When Queen Victoria came to the throne in 1837: "Larne was only a quiet town in an out-of-the-way corner of Ireland. But it had a harbour, and by 1865, in spite of delays and disappointments, roads had been improved, the railway had arrived, and the feasibility of providing a short sea steam-driven service to Britain had been demonstrated. Larne was on its way towards becoming the important entrepot which nature had designed it to be. But, apart from developing as the Irish end of the short sea passage, Larne had difficulty finding an economic role for itself. Should it be an industrial centre, a market town or a seaside resort – or all three? Its small industries, of which bleaching and flour milling were the most important, had to compete with larger rivals in nearby Belfast. The new Market Place, created in 1864, helped traders, but could not fully compensate for a comparatively meagre hinterland. . . ."[6]

James Chaine, however, soon demonstrated his qualities as an entrepreneur and in so doing he gave the town a sense of purpose and a new lease of life. From his early days he appeared to have shown keen business acumen. He was singled out for special mention in the 1861 will of his grandfather William Chaine, who had become rich through the linen business. "I request and hope that my business may be carried on by my son Wm Chaine and my said grandson James Chaine, said James taking and assuming my place as principal, and my son Wm taking part therein as he has heretofore done with myself."

However, William Chaine later displeased his father who added a codicil to his will thus: "(since some months back) said Wm Chaine has altogether neglected any attendance on the business and absented himself from Muckamore Bleaching and Linen business, I NOW DECLARE that said Wm Chaine my son shall not enter into attendance on said business, but shall have his annuity paid after my death without any share in the profits thereof, nor will he be liable for any share of losses thereon." Old man Chaine's displeasure with his son William was nothing compared to that over his other son John, who made a brief appearance in the original will as follows: "To my son the Reverend John Chaine I leave the sum of £5 stg and no more."[7] William Chaine died "on or about the 21st day of July 1862", without making any more amendments to his will.

We can only guess at the reason for such parental wrath – was it John's refusal to take part in the family business, was it profligacy while in the cloth, was it a bitter and unresolved quarrel between parent and child, or did the father believe that his religious son would receive his reward in Heaven? Notwithstanding such speculation, the point remains that James Chaine showed early enterprise and was given a clear run in the family business. This would have provided him with valuable experience as he set out to revolutionise Larne Harbour, for that is essentially what he achieved in a short space of time.

From his arrival in Larne in 1866 Chaine lost no time in getting down to business. "Over the period of the next two years Chaine had the original pier, harbour and quays repaired. Following an advertisement in the Belfast News Letter of 13 May 1867, seeking applications for tenders for the construction of a Timber Pier at Curran, Larne, the contract was awarded to Kent and Smith of Belfast at a price of £1,403-16-2. The new pier was 160 feet long, about 32 feet wide and at low tide there was 19 feet of water. In 1872 the quays were extended to the south of the harbour and the shore behind filled in. Gregg and Company, Belfast, obtained this contract, the price being £8,569-10-0."[8]

The foreign trade, according to the Harbour Master's entry book for the years 1867-75, consisted almost entirely of wheat, and most of the export trade was iron ore, shipped in small schooners averaging some 50 tons. The Bank Quays handled most of the coasting trade and almost all of the coal trade, with only a few coal cargoes being discharged at the harbour.[9] James Chaine's major priority was to re-establish a sea-link with Scotland, but he needed the co-operation of the Scottish authorities. In 1871 the Larne and Stranraer Steamboat Company was formed, with nominal capital of £20,000 in £10 shares. The money on the Irish side came from private sponsors, including directors of the Belfast and Northern Counties Railway and the Carrickfergus and Larne Railway, and James Chaine himself, who invested £1,000. A new paddle steamer, the Princess Louise, a 497 ton vessel built by Tod and McGregor of Glasgow, was bought for £18,500 and commenced a regular service between Larne and Stranraer on 1 July 1872.[10]

In a series of daylight sailings the vessel left Stranraer at 10 am and returned from Larne at 5 pm. According to one writer she was, for those days, a "state of the art" ship. "Princess Louise was built to the highest standards for passenger comfort. The accommodation for cabin passengers was situated aft, with a saloon, a smoke-room and a state-room. The decor was in true, heavy Victorian style. The panelling of the walls and ceiling of the saloon were painted in imitation satin wood and the cornicing consisted of gilt cable with pendant medallions of the Royal lady whose name the vessel bore. (Princess Louise, the Marchioness of Lorne, was the daughter of Queen Victoria.) The gable panes of the deck lights for the saloon were adorned with stained glass representations of the Marquis and Marchioness of Lorne. The bows, stern and paddle boxes were decorated with shields bearing the arms of Argyll, heraldic insignia and enlarged medallions alto relievo portraits of the Marquis and Marchioness, the latter surmounted by a royal coronet. Steerage accommodation, with wooden benches, was provided forward, and it was claimed to equal the cabin accommodation of many ships then plying. Space for cattle was also forward."[11]

The Princess Louise started well, and in her first three months 4,561 passengers were carried, as well as 202 horses and 6,349 cattle.[12]

The *Larne Weekly Reporter* of 24 August 1872 was most enthusiastic: "Although the short-sea service between Larne and Stranraer has only been in existence since the first of July last, the amount of traffic has been very great, and is steadily increasing. This route is rapidly becoming popular, and once the superior advantages possessed by the service become more generally known, it cannot fail to have the effect of still further attracting the attention of the travelling community on this, and on our sister isle. When once the extensive wharves are completed, which are being constructed by James Chaine Esq, at the Corran, this route will be one of the most complete between Ireland and Great Britain. The New Line of railway in course of formation between Stranraer and Girvan, and which will be finished at the end of the present year, will shorten the distance between Belfast and Glasgow by about two hours and a half."

After so many setbacks, it appeared that the route was at last fulfilling its potential, but the Princess Louise needed frequent overhauls, and other vessels, including the paddle steamer Albion, had to be chartered to cover the service. It soon became clear, however, that another ship was needed. The Princess Beatrice was ordered from Harland and Wolff in Belfast for £24,000 and launched at the Queen's Yard on 4 November 1875. In February 1876 she took over from the Princess Louise, which was again out of commission, and after a shaky start (during which the Princess Louise provided cover), the two vessels began to provide a more reliable service.

A mail route was established from 1875, after the disappointments of the past, and mail from the north of England and Scotland was transported to Ireland via Larne, and vice versa. (A Post Office contract for £30 per annum had been awarded to the Carrickfergus and Larne line in 1865, and in 1884 some parcel mail from London moved through Stranraer, but it was not until 1891 that letter mail was used on this route to a significant degree.)[13]

Meanwhile, James Chaine turned his attention to the extension of the railway link to Larne, as this was part of the life-blood of the port. Because of the hilly hinterland around the town, access was difficult, particularly with horse-drawn traffic. Chaine favoured a rail link through central Antrim, but the first plan for a line to Antrim town was abandoned in 1873. In November of the same year there was a Belfast meeting of shareholders to establish a Larne and Ballyclare Railway Company. James Chaine, as ever to the fore, was the principal shareholder, subscribing £5,000.

It was decided, however, that the line should continue to Ballymena, and the name was changed to the Ballymena-Larne Narrow Gauge Railway. The line was authorised by Act of Parliament in 1874, and work on the Larne-Ballyclare section was not started until 1876, due to lack of funds. However, goods traffic began to use this section from September 1877, and the total length to Ballymena was in use for passengers and freight by the end of August the next year. However, the Larne-Ballymena line did not link up with the Belfast and Northern Counties Railway at Ballymena until 1880.[14]

Not content with establishing new rail and sea links for Larne, James Chaine also turned his attention to politics and in February 1874, he was elected as an MP to the Westminster Parliament. One contemporary account in the Larne Weekly Reporter of 21 February captured the sense of local excitement at the election of this popular and dynamic businessman. It noted that: "Crowds had congregated in the vicinity of the Post Office in Larne to hear the result announced and when it became clear that Chaine had been elected there was vociferous cheering. Around 10 o'clock a large party appeared on the scene accompanied with fifes and drums and a parade took place around the town. When the parade reached the Conservative committee rooms [wherever they may have been], cheers were given for the successful candidates, the election committee, Mr WW McNeill, Conservative agent, and several other gentlemen who had taken a prominent part in the election and helped secure the return of Messrs Chaine and O'Neill as MPs. Tar barrels were also lighted in the town and in elevated parts of the area. About eleven o'clock a large number left Larne for nearby Cairncastle, where Chaine resided, and a large bell used for calling servants and labourers was rung to summon everyone in the neighbourhood to hear the news. The celebrations apparently went on until 4 am in the morning, and there were also victory festivities at Magheramorne, where about 400 people were headed by a parade of local Orangemen to a field where tar barrels and bonfires were lit, and burned for about two hours. The crowd then adjourned to the schoolroom nearby, where the evening was brought to a conclusion by singing, aided by Mr Hugh Beggs and William Grant of Larne. In the port of Larne itself, meanwhile, the State Line ship 'State of Virginia', bedecked in flags, fired a four gun salute as she sailed into Larne the day after the election result."[15]

As well as being a most successful and popular businessman, Chaine was also something of a character. WD Morrow, a former Agricultural Editor of the Belfast Telegraph and a well-known character himself in his heyday, recalled some of Chaine's eccentricities. "James Chaine had his own particular way of pulling humanity's leg. He collected clocks, and had scores of them all over the house. There were 'chimers' and 'strikers' – and some too, which gave out the quarter-hour chimes. He entertained well and disliked his guests hurrying away at midnight, so he devised a method of detaining them; it was a simple one. He set his clocks at different hours and had them chiming and striking in such a way that no one in the house could tell the correct time. While the hospitality went on and James Chaine appeared the perfect host, he was quietly having his own little 'leg pull'. He drew plenty of amusement from the frustration of his guests in trying to tell the time. If a guest pulled out a watch and looked at 'the time', he would confound the guest by asking him to look at the clock in the hall, which he had, of course, previously carefully altered. Undoubtedly, Mr Chaine would convince him that he was hurrying off home far too early.

"The late Dr Norman Graham, who lived in a lovely house further along the road near Islandbawn, once told me some of the stories relating to Mr Chaine. These he had heard from his father, and other friends of the early days, of the old house and the Chaine family. James Chaine also loved horses, and when the railway was first laid between Belfast and Antrim, he sometimes awaited the arrival of the 'up-train' at Ballycraigy gates, and would then drive furiously in his carriage to Dunadry Station a few miles away, in a race with the train."[16]

Given the popularity and the eminence of such a man, it is not difficult to imagine the sense of shock at James Chaine's untimely death, from pneumonia, at the age of 44. It was described by a Mr Miles at the Borough Council meeting of 4 May 1885 as "A sad and sudden calamity that the town and vicinity has suffered . . ." The Ballymena Observer carried the story, and despite the characteristically overblown style of reportage in Victorian times, the profound sadness and dismay at Chaine's death is inescapable: "It was with the most unfeigned sorrow and regret that the inhabitants of Ballymena heard of the death of Mr James Chaine on Monday morning last. The sad event took place at the Olderfleet Hotel, Larne, after a very acute attack of inflammation of the lungs, occasioned by a cold contracted at Larne Harbour on Monday, 27 April, making preparations to give the Prince (later King Edward VII) and Princess of Wales a suitable reception. On that day Mr Chaine was ubiquitous, and did not seem to be able to do half enough for the reception of the Royal visitors or the accommodation of the public and by his personal exertions made the departure of the Prince and Princess from our shores one of the most enjoyable episodes of the Royal visit. On the following day (Tuesday) the deceased felt a chill, and Dr Austin, Larne, was called in to see him, and subsequently Doctors JW Smith Cuming and Gaussen were consulted, and all was done that skill and experience could suggest. Up till Sunday no particular change was noticed, but on Monday morning he began to sink rapidly, and passed away at about eight o'clock, in presence of those who tenderly watched at his bedside.

A Robert Welch photograph of the Olderfleet Hotel, where James Chaine died in 1885 at the untimely age of 44. He developed pneumonia after catching a cold at the harbour on 27 April. His death was described at the local Council as 'A sad and sudden calamity that the town has suffered'.

Courtesy of the Ulster Museum W01/67/10

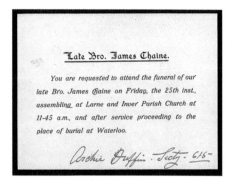

A notice to Thomas Robinson Esq. to attend the funeral of 'Bro. James Chaine' who was Conservative MP for Larne at the Westminster Parliament.

When his death became known in Larne there was the deepest regret felt by everyone, for all realised that something like a calamity had happened to that improving seaport. Business places were partially closed, and colours flying from buildings and ships in the harbour were lowered to half mast high. . . . Although a Conservative in politics, he did not carry his political opinions into his private life. Indeed, his politics were of a very independent type, and we would venture to say that he was quite as popular with many of his political opponents as he could have been if he had been a most pronounced Liberal. About Larne his name will ever be associated with the magnificent harbour he has constructed, and the business he has drawn to the port; and from Ballymena to Larne the narrow-gauge railway will be a lasting memorial of his genius and ability. It is arranged that his funeral will take place from the Olderfleet Hotel on this day (Friday), at twelve o'clock."

The Ulster Echo's appreciation was concise and to the point: "His death will cause universal regret in the county and wherever he was known, for Mr Chaine was one of those kindly, genial, and generous men who make friends everywhere. He inherited a fine estate and some valuable manufactories, and had he been content to rest and be thankful, he might have enjoyed a life of indolent ease. But he was not of that kind. He was a man of great energy and enterprise, and laboured more than most men for the prosperity of the county with which his interests were bound up. The remarkable development of the town and harbour of Larne is the result of Mr Chaine's sleepless energy, and both will long remain as monuments of his anxious care and restless enterprise. The important position which Larne has attained, and the still more important position it is destined to attain as a highway to America and England, is entirely owing to Mr Chaine's enterprise and attention, and the inhabitants for whom he has done so much should long cherish his memory with affectionate regard. The narrow gauge railway to Ballymena may be also said to be the offspring of his own enterprise, and he took more pride and pleasure in these public achievements than many men would have done in undertakings that ministered to their own personal comfort or gratification. He never considered the time nor the money wasted that was devoted to the improvement and development of Larne. Unhappily, he did not survive to reap the fruit of his years of labour and thought."

James Chaine remained original to the end – it is said that one of his last requests was to be buried looking out to sea, in a standing position, and wearing his naval attire. "He was interred, as he had requested, in what is now Chaine Park at the Bank Heads. The burial ground, in which his widow and sons – who died without issue – now also rest, is tastefully enclosed in a railed area, and diligently cared for by Larne Borough Council."[17]

The citizens of Larne and district lost little time in setting about to create a suitable monument. The Ballymena Observer of 23 May 1885 reported: "A largely-attended meeting, convened by circular, was held in the McGarel Town Hall, Larne, for the purpose of initiating a movement to erect a memorial in memory of the late Mr Chaine MP. Captain McCalmont occupied the Chair. . . . The Chairman eulogised Mr Chaine as a gentleman who possessed the best qualities, not only of a private friend, but of a public benefactor. To him they owed much of the prosperity of the County Antrim. They were going to suggest to the friends of Mr Chaine that they should form themselves into committees at various places, and when the time came it could be decided as to what form the memorial should assume.

Somewhat eccentric in life, James Chaine was also eccentric in death – it is said that one of his last requests was to be buried in a standing position, looking out to sea, and wearing his naval attire. These pictures show the commanding views across the Channel, with Scotland clearly visible on a clear day (above left). The simple Gravestones are those of Chaine and his family (above right).

Photos: Alf McCreary

"Lord O'Neill moved the following resolution: 'That in the opinion of this meeting it is most desirable that immediate steps be taken to place on record the recognition of the services of the late Mr Chaine, MP for the County of Antrim, during the eleven years he was the senior member, of his many works of enterprise undertaken with the view of furthering the prosperity of his native county, and of his numerous acts of public and private charity; and, consequently, it is now determined by his many friends to erect a memorial to his memory, in a manner hereafter to be determined on, and to be known as the Chaine Memorial.' He might say that Mr Chaine had reared his own monument, and to whom could well be applied the terms of the inscription in St Paul's, which referred to Sir Christopher Wren, 'If you seek a monument, look around.' (Applause.) But they (his friends) wanted something to be done to perpetuate the knowledge of his genial, manly, and friendly qualities.

"Mr John Owens, JP (Holestone), seconded the resolution, which was unanimously carried.

"Rev Francis Young then moved, and Mr H McNeill seconded the following resolution: 'That a committee be appointed, with power to add to their number, with a view to carrying out the objects of the foregoing resolution, and that Mr William Eccles and

Mr Charles Howden, jun, of Larne, be appointed hon secs to the committee.' The motion was unanimously passed.

"Mr James Macauley moved, and Mr Alex Williams seconded, the following, which was also passed – 'That the friends of the late Mr Chaine be invited to form committees in various districts of the County of Antrim to further the success of the Chaine Memorial, and that such committees forward to the hon secs the names of those desirous of joining the general committee.'

"Rev JB Meek proposed the following – 'That a subscription list, to close on 1 July next, be now opened, and that the thanks of this meeting be tendered to the Belfast, Northern and Ulster Banks, who have consented to receive subscriptions and act as treasurers to the Chaine Memorial Fund.'" (Despite such high-mindedness, the citizens were also concerned with the early business of politics, and the same edition of the newspaper reported that the nomination of candidates for the Westminster seat left vacant by Mr Chaine's death had already taken place!)

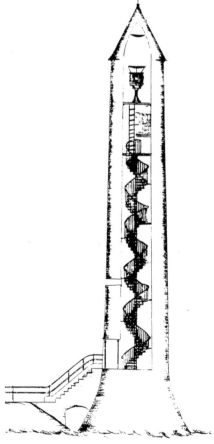

An architect's impression of the inside of the tower

Courtesy of the Journal of the Irish Lighthouse Service

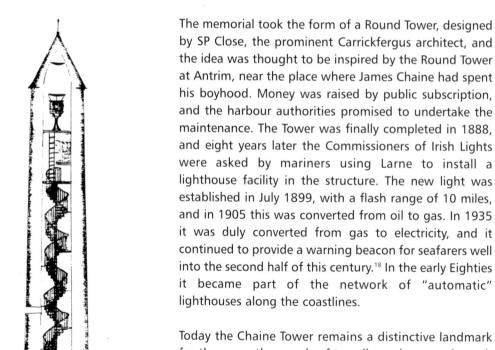

The memorial took the form of a Round Tower, designed by SP Close, the prominent Carrickfergus architect, and the idea was thought to be inspired by the Round Tower at Antrim, near the place where James Chaine had spent his boyhood. Money was raised by public subscription, and the harbour authorities promised to undertake the maintenance. The Tower was finally completed in 1888, and eight years later the Commissioners of Irish Lights were asked by mariners using Larne to install a lighthouse facility in the structure. The new light was established in July 1899, with a flash range of 10 miles, and in 1905 this was converted from oil to gas. In 1935 it was duly converted from gas to electricity, and it continued to provide a warning beacon for seafarers well into the second half of this century.[18] In the early Eighties it became part of the network of "automatic" lighthouses along the coastlines.

Today the Chaine Tower remains a distinctive landmark for the many thousands of travellers who pass through the port each year, and the sight of the Irish Round Tower is both a reminder of home to locals and also an appropriate introduction for outsiders, to this distinctive region of the British Isles. On a clear, sunny day the foreshore near the Tower provides a fine vantage point to watch the shipping arrive at and leave the Port of Larne – many of the vessels using the aptly-

named Chaine Quay as their berth. And as one looks across the Lough and observes the various Captains manoeuvring their huge craft, it is hard not to remark on the huge advances in seafaring technology and transport since James Chaine's day and to recognise the huge debt which the port owes to this remarkable man of vision and enterprise.

The Tower itself has a fitting inscription: "THIS TOWER was erected and the ROAD leading to it made by the contributions of every class in this mixed community, irrespective of creed or party, all cordially united in esteem and affection for the memory of James Chaine of Ballycraigy and Cairncastle, Co Antrim, who represented this county in the Imperial Parliament of Great Britain and Ireland from February 1874 till 4 May 1885 when his early and lamented death in the 44th year of his age deprived his native county of one who had worked indefatigably for its interests especially in developing and improving the natural capabilities of the Harbour of Larne, and establishing its connection with Great Britain and the United States of America and with the inland part of this County."

The Chaine Memorial Tower, which dominates the entrance to the Port of Larne. The design was inspired by the Round Tower in Antrim, near the place where James Chaine had spent his boyhood. Up to the present time, it has been used as a Lighthouse. This Valentine view of Larne shows the Chaine Tower on the left, the Bankheads complete with seaside strollers, and ladies and gentlemen's bathing boxes – but not together!

Courtesy of an early brochure published by John Fullerton of Larne and printed by Valentine & Sons Ltd., Dundee.

A somewhat less elegant but nevertheless heartfelt tribute to James Chaine was written by a WJ Saunders of Belfast in July 1886, in the form of a poem about his grave. The poem was published in the Larne Reporter:

"Yes, there he sleeps, a Hero sleeps
Beneath the rising mound,
Where sky and sea their vigils keep
Upon the hallowed ground.

Fit emblems, these, of one whose life
Illumines history's page,
Whose deeds of kindness and of love
Shall pass from age to age.

Equalled by few, excelled by none
And though beneath the sod,
He leaves full many a grateful heart
To bless the paths he trod.

And Friendship too, her tribute pays
Unto his priceless worth,
For Larne has a memorial raised
The best in all the North.

And as we gaze upon the spot
So beautiful and grand,
Our hearts are filled with love for him
Who loved his native land.

For few to Larne such friendship gave
Or ever will again,
An aching void must now be felt
Where once he used to reign.

All honour be to such as he
And though removed far,
From active life to dreamless sleep
Yet in our hearts he's near.

Long, long may he be cherished
Long be his memory green,
A truer heart ne'er was entombed
A better man ne'er seen."

1. From historical documents in the possession of Larne Harbour Ltd.
2. Ibid.
3. Op.Cit. RH McIlrath, pp109-110, with reference to attributed sources.
4. Ibid, p118.
5. Ibid, p116.
6. Ibid, p133.
7. References to William Chaine's Will are extracted from the Probate and Matrimonial Division of the High Court of Justice, Ireland, in the District Registry of Belfast 1861.
8. Op.Cit. Jane M Ludlow, pp62-63, with reference to Capt W Close in "The Development of Larne Harbour: 1867-1873 in The Corran, Vol I" (Larne 1976 pp6-7).
9. "History of Larne Harbour" by David J McNeilly, p29, Larne 1957.
10. Op.Cit. Jane M Ludlow, pp63-64.
11. Op.Cit. Fraser G MacHaffie, p66.
12. Ibid, p67.
13. Ibid, p72.
14. Op.Cit. Jane M Ludlow, p69, and relevant sources.
15. "The History Corner" by Dr David Hume, Larne Times, 28 February 1991.
16. East Antrim Times, 18 July 1975.
17. "The Chaine Memorial Tower" by WR Hamilton, p17, Printed in BEAM, the Journal of the Irish Lighthouse Service, Vol XVIII, No. 1, December 1989
18. Mrs M Close "The Corran" No. 42 Spring Edition, Published by the Larne and District Folklore Society.

A Robert Welch study of the liner
State of Nebraska.

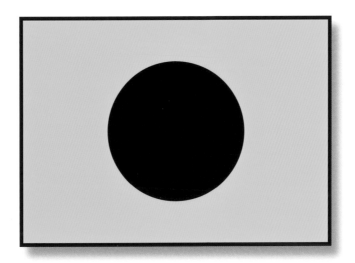

CHAPTER 3

TOWARDS THE NEW CENTURY

Two days before his untimely death on 4 May 1885, James Chaine signed his Last Will and Testament, which was legally witnessed by his family physician Dr JJ Austin and the family solicitor Charles H Brett. He appointed as Executors his son William, and his trusted business colleague Donald Macdonald, who was to play an important role in the further development of Larne harbour.

Specifically, the dying James Chaine left instructions that Donald Macdonald should take "immediate possession of all papers in the tin boxes and despatch boxes in the billiard room of my house at Ballycraigy, and also all papers and articles in the drawers in my own dressing-room at Ballycraigy, and also all papers in the boxes, drawers and bags in the room known as the 'Tower Room' at Ballycraigy. I direct that the said Donald Macdonald shall in his sole and uncontrolled discretion dispose of all said papers and articles as he shall think fit, and he may destroy all or any of them as he thinks right, subject to any charges affecting my property at my death and to the provisions for my wife and for my son James hereinafter contained."[1]

James Chaine directed that his son William, to whom he left the major part of his estate, should finish his education at Cambridge "before attaining the age of 25", or as he and Mr Macdonald thought best, but that, significantly, he should learn the business at Larne Harbour under the direction of Macdonald, who was to be paid "a clear sum of one thousand pounds a year." James Chaine also provided a legacy of £20,000 for his other son, also called James, but right to the very end of his life he demonstrated his strong conviction about the future prosperity of Larne. He decreed that 'if and when Larne Harbour shall turn out as I have always expected it would – a great commercial success – I desire that William should pay James a further sum of £10,000 in addition to the £20,000 hereinbefore bequeathed, if William and Donald Macdonald think that such should be done, but not otherwise."[2]

James Chaine's optimism about Larne was not misplaced, and the port gradually prospered, though not without much hard work and certain teething troubles. The stock of the main backers "had yielded no dividend by 1889 and, when approached by the Directors, the 55 private investors from Ireland agreed to sell their stock at £6-5-0 per £10 share. At a Board meeting of the Larne and Stranraer Steamboat Company the motion was adopted to wind up the existing company and establish a new and larger one. The new company took over all the liabilities of the old company, paid off loans and purchased the shares held by the Irish shareholders. It also took over the assets, including the two ships. At this meeting a sub-committee was set up to obtain designs and prices for a new steamer for the route. Messrs William Denny & Bros, of Dumbarton, won the contract to build the 'Princess Victoria' at a cost of £46,000. The 1096 ton ship was a steel paddle steamer, 280 feet long, with a speed of 18 knots, consuming 2 3/4 tons of coal per hour. On 1 May 1890, the new ship took over from the 'Princess Louise' which was sold for £2,250. The 'Princess Victoria' was faster and much more reliable than the other ships. During the summer of 1890 she made two round trips per day and more than 10,000 passengers used the daylight service."[3]

The new Princess Victoria was a remarkable vessel for her time. As the redoubtable Fraser G MacHaffie notes in his detailed study The Short Sea Route: "In all respects Princess Victoria introduced new standards to the Stranraer route. She was fitted with electric light and, contrary to the usual practice in paddle steamers, saloon accommodation was provided amidships and in the forward region of the ship. On the upper deck, between the funnels, four private cabins, each with accommodation for two, were provided as an innovation. In the same area there was a large cabin for ladies, while forward of the funnels there was a beautifully upholstered general cabin. Ample accommodation was provided, we are told, below the forecastle for deck passengers.

"Special provision was made for the carrying of livestock, and seven hundred cattle could be accommodated, as well as a number of horses. The elaborate scale of the accommodation was possible because of the greater size of the 'Victoria' when compared with her two older consorts. She was 70 feet longer than the 'Louise', and using gross tonnage as a rough and ready indication of enclosed accommodation, the 'Victoria's 1,096 contrasts with the 497 for the 'Louise' and 556 for the 'Beatrice'. Alongside concern for the comfort of the passengers we see a developing concern for their safety, and Princess Victoria was built with seven water-tight bulkheads all carried up to main deck level."[4]

Unfortunately, the Princess Victoria, like her successors of the same name, was dogged by misfortune. On her first day in service she ran into a schooner, causing considerable damage to the other vessel, and she was continually beset by weather and mechanical difficulties. On 4 June 1891 she was disabled some ten miles from Larne when her port wheel struck floating wreckage, and she was

The State Line vessel State of Indiana, 1882. This trans-Atlantic service between Glasgow, Larne and New York began in 1873 and lasted until December 1889, though there were sailings between Glasgow and New York for some time afterwards. Many hundreds of emigrants left Larne to start a new life in America.

An 1887 picture by Robert Welch of the liner State of Georgia, taken from Islandmagee. Of equal interest is the apparel of the local inhabitants facing the camera, and the conditions of their home.

RW169

ignominiously towed into Larne. A letter-writer to the Belfast News Letter praised the coolness of her Master, John McCracken. After he had determined the damage, he stood back and slowly lit his pipe, an action which apparently calmed the passengers![5]

An important boost for Larne was the offer of a Post Office mail contract of £8,000 per annum for the steamship section, after many years of discussion. It began on 1 September 1891, and the route's operators proved conclusively that they could handle the mail efficiently. Four years later a satisfactory report was made to Parliament, underlining the punctuality of the service. However, one major requirement of the contract was the availability of suitable vessels, including a stand-by ship. The Princess Beatrice, which was to be sold off, was retained for another 12 years as the standby, while either of the two other vessels were absent for overhaul, or otherwise out of service. In May 1892 the Princess May, a replica of the Victoria costing £47,000, joined the route, and both vessels – with the backup of the Princess Beatrice – provided a regular, and largely reliable, service well into the new Century.[6]

There were, however, a number of mishaps which were not without humour – as recalled by Fraser G MacHaffie:

"Princess Victoria left Larne with some three hundred passengers on the morning run on Saturday, 3 September 1892, and once outside the harbour felt the full force of a gale. All went well until the ship was nearly within the shelter of Loch Ryan, when Chief Engineer Henderson was forced to stop the engines following a great crashing in the port paddle box. He discovered that one of the outer arms had broken and this left a paddle float hanging loose. Normally it would have been a simple job to disconnect completely the float, but in the gale this was impossible. Captain McCracken dropped anchor and the ship swung to in Port Mullen Bay, near Corsewall Point. Distress signals were sent up. The lighthouse at Corsewall Point failed to see these, but they were seen in Ballantrae and the lifeboat launched. Also a telegram was sent to the railway office at Stranraer.

"The lifeboat was half-way to the 'Victoria' when the crew saw a ship approaching the disabled paddler and they headed into the shelter of Loch Ryan. The ship approaching the 'Victoria' was the tug Gamecock and the master of the tug offered to tow Princess Victoria to Stranraer for £300. Captain McCracken would not go above £250. Gamecock lay off to see if resistance would break down, but, before long, smoke of another ship was seen heading for Port Mullen. Captain Campbell, on board the 'Victoria's' younger sister at Larne, had received word of the accident and brought Princess May over. Captain Campbell dropped anchor and allowed the 'May' to swing round to within sixty feet of her sister. A boat was launched and a rope passed from the 'May' to the 'Victoria'. Gamecock lingered for a short time to see if there might be any pickings, but soon headed off in a cloud of smoke!"

On another occasion, "the Princess Victoria was sent off to Larne around 21.00 with passengers and mail that the 'May' should have taken. About 23.30 the 'Victoria' left Larne to make contact with her sister and, if required, tow her back to the mainland. In the darkness the 'Victoria' missed the 'May', which by now had drifted in towards the Ayrshire coast. Around midnight Cairnryan had passed to Stranraer a message from a shepherd, 'Ship at anchor under Bennane Head and a lot of hammering'. The shepherd, sensing something was amiss, had walked some eight miles to deliver the message. He was later to receive a gift of £5 from the steamboat company. Eventually the 'May' managed to get under way and arrived back at Stranraer about lunchtime on the following day – eighteen hours late. Princess May was taken to Dumbarton for repairs and the 'Victoria' maintained the double service single-handed for the remaining four days of the summer timetable."[7]

Meanwhile, a new limited liability company was formed at Larne to deal with the increasing business. On 26 November 1891 the first meeting of the so-called "Old Company" – Larne Harbour Ltd – was held "at the offices of L'Estrange and Brett, 9 Chichester Street, Belfast when there were present Chas H Brett, William Chaine and D Macdonald. "It was resolved that two directors should form a quorum, and also that all cheques drawn by the company or endorsements to or from them are negotiable with the signature of one Managing Director. The following appointees were made. Secretary to the Company John McDowell, Collector of Rates Hugh O'Brien."[8] This company remained in existence until 1912, when a new company was formed.

The Larne-Stranraer crossing became the dominant route, but there were a number of others operating out of Larne from the middle of the 19th century. "From 1865 until around 1900 the Laird Line, sailing between Portrush and Liverpool, called at Larne. The Ayr Steam Shipping Company had three sailings per week in each direction between Ayr and Larne in 1866; these were halted after a short period but were revived ten years later. In January 1877 the locally owned 'Larne' commenced a tri-weekly passenger-cargo service between Larne and Glasgow. G&J Burns of Glasgow, set up in competition against the 'Larne' in August 1878, offering a twice weekly cargo and passenger service by the 'Rook' and about six months later the 'Larne' was withdrawn. After a short period the 'Rook' ceased to carry passengers but continued to transport cargo for at least the next thirty years."[9]

By 1881, other services were operating once a week to Ballina, Campbeltown, Londonderry, Dublin and Liverpool, and the Belfast, Bangor and Larne Steamboat Co Ltd operated from all three ports from 1877 to circa 1894. The local ferry service to Islandmagee operated virtually on demand, and although there were complaints in 1867 about the inadequate facilities for landing, despite the new wharves, these were quickly remedied.[10]

An advertisement in the "AF Guide and Directory 1888, County Antrim" gives some of the flavour of the life of the contemporary harbour, as a bustling sea-port:

"Ballymena and Larne Railway
Is the shortest route from Ballymena and Ballyclare to the port of Larne, and goods can be booked at same through rates to Scotch and English Stations as via Belfast. The railway wagons run alongside the vessels, and goods are taken out of the vessels, and placed in the wagons by the cranes.

Steamers from Larne (To Glasgow calling at Greenock)
Every Tuesday and Friday, and from Glasgow and Greenock to Larne every Monday and Thursday, carrying passengers, cattle and goods in connection with Scotch Railways.

To and From Stranraer
Every weekday carrying passengers, mails, livestock and goods for England and Scotland. Sea passage, two hours. Loch sailing forty minutes.

To Ayr
On Tuesdays, Thursdays and Saturdays, and from Ayr to Larne on Mondays, Wednesdays and Fridays carrying goods in connection with Glasgow and South Western Railway. Through rates between Glasgow, Paisley, Govan, Renfrew, Johnstone, and Ayr and Ballymena.

To Liverpool
On Tuesdays and Saturdays, and from Liverpool to Larne on Mondays and Thursdays. For hours of sailing see Bills; carrying passengers, livestock and goods at through rates between English Stations and Ballyclare and Ballymena.

To New York
State Line every Saturday, carrying passengers and goods. Agents, Geo C Pim and Co, Larne Harbour.

For particulars of rates &c apply to Ballymena & Larne Ry Co, Ballymena.

It was the advent of the State Line in 1873, however, which caused the greatest stir of excitement by inaugurating a passenger and cargo service between Larne and New York, with the vessels arriving at Larne from Glasgow. This carried on the tradition of emigration which had been established in the previous century.

A picture of Larne Harbour c. 1889 showing a State Line steamer (left) and a timber barque alongside the quays. The platform for the railway had been built (middle left and right) prior to the erection of the railway station itself. Given the elevation, it is likely that the photograph was taken from an upstairs floor of the Olderfleet Hotel.

During the extensive 18th Century emigration by the Ulster-Scots to North America, the first emigrant ship to sail from Larne was the Friend's Goodwill, which embarked from the harbour – originally at Quay Street – in early May, 1717. After a long voyage marked by both storm and calm, it arrived safely in Boston in September of that year. Thousands of Ulster emigrants sailed principally to New York, Philadelphia and Charleston.

The Ulster-American Blue Plaque Heritage Trail, established by an Ulster-American Committee set up by Larne Borough Council in 1992, traces the rich and varied associations between the port and the emigrants. According to literature prepared by Dr David Hume for the Ulster-American Committee "between July 1771 and September 1772, there were at least seven sailings from the port, all but one to Charleston. They involved the ships Jupiter, James and Mary, Betty, and Lord Dunluce. It is estimated that they took over 1,700 passengers, hoping for better fortunes in America."

The Ulster-American Heritage Trail features no fewer than 14 plaques dotted around the Larne Borough, commemorating such diverse figures as the Reverend Dr James Boyd Brady, a leading Methodist cleric in and around Boston in the latter part of the 19th century; Bishop James Augustine McFaul, who in 1894 became Roman Catholic Bishop of Trenton, New

Jersey; General Sam Houston, the first President of Texas; and Theodore Roosevelt, the President of the United States from 1901-1909, whose Ulster-Scots ancestors hailed from the village of Gleno, near Larne. The strong connection between Larne and emigration to North America is tangibly represented by an impressive Memorial to the Emigrants, in Curran Park. Cast in bronze, it was designed by sculptor Ed Barton on the advice of the Ulster-American Committee, and unveiled in May 1992 by Dr Bobby Moss of Blacksburg, South Carolina, a noted authority on the role of the Ulster-Scots in the American Revolution.

The Larne Reporter provided a comprehensive overview of emigration from the port in the 18th century:

"About the middle of last century, there was also a very brisk emigration trade at Larne, carried on by a fleet of emigrant ships which then regularly left our port for America. Indeed at that time Larne was almost the only port in the North of Ireland from which emigrant vessels sailed. In 1754, three of these vessels – viz, the ship 'William and George', the snow 'Antrim', and the sloop 'Vaughan' – sailed from Larne with passengers for America, the average number being 300 in each vessel.

"In the Belfast News Letter of 5 March 1760, 'the snow Captain Breton mounting 10 guns and men answerable, commanded by Captain Robert Wilson', was advertised to sail from Larne for New York, the 1st April ensuing, wind and weather permitting. 'Any who inclined to indent as servants, go on redemption as passengers, or had goods to ship on freight, were to apply to Mr George Dunlop, of Ballycastle, Captain John Wisnom, or Mr Hugh Montgomery, of Larne, or Mr Thomas Greg, of Belfast.' In 1771 AD, two ships sailed from Larne for America with 450 passengers.

"In 1772 AD, five ships (three for Charleston and two for New York) took from our harbour to the same place 1,300 passengers, and in 1773, a similar number were conveyed in four vessels, the number of passengers being in each case computed to be almost equal to the tonnage of each vessel. These people were generally of a superior class to those who had previously left Ireland. They were mostly weavers, small farmers, or persons of some little property – in almost every instance they paid their own passage money on this side (which amounted to £3 10s 0d each), and were not ranked out by their friends in America.

"It was calculated that one ship had no less than £4,000 in specie, on board. On 16 January 1796, 'the brigantine Sally of Savanna, burthen 300 tons, Isaac Gedney, master', was advertised to sail from Larne, for Charleston and Savanna, on the first of March next ensuing – referring for freight or passage to agents in Belfast, Coagh, Loughbrickland, Ballymena, Cookstown and Larne, and especially to 'Mr Muir, one of the owners of the vessel, at his lodgings in Larne, who had it in his power to give a great deal of useful information to such persons as might wish to take their passage or send goods in the Sally." (Published on 23 December 1871.)

The first State Line vessel to visit Larne was the SS State of Pennsylvania. Ian Duffin, a Larne man whose grandfather was a bosun on the State Line's SS Nebraska, remembers his father

talking about the days when he and his uncle used to go down to the harbour with his grandfather's supplies for the Atlantic crossing, including his bedding and a supply of bread. Ian Duffin, who has made an extensive study of the subject, wrote a detailed outline for the Larne Guardian of 18 December 1991.

Referring to the inaugural visit of the SS State of Pennsylvania, he noted: "19 April was a great day in Larne. A large number of the townspeople and those from the surrounding countryside were at the harbour for the event. The workhouse band was on the Curran, playing the popular airs of the day, and Henry McNeill's wagonettes and side cars loaded to capacity, plied all day between the town and the harbour.

"State Line officials had investigated and reported on the suitability of Larne Harbour to accommodate their vessels before commencing the service. This was fortunate for James Chaine, for about five years later, the owners of a vessel claimed damages which, they said, occurred when their vessel was lying alongside at Larne Harbour. Mr Chaine won the case on every point, principally on the evidence of the State Line officials who had inspected the berths in 1873."

A panoramic view by Robert Welch of the Curran and Larne Harbour circa 1890. In the background (right) a State Line ship lies alongside the quay, and the American 'Stars and Stripes' flutters above the Olderfleet Hotel on the left. Next to the hotel the two-storey house, now the offices of Larne Harbour Ltd, seems in excellent condition.

Courtesy of the Ulster Museum WOI/67/9

However, not everyone shared the euphoria surrounding the inauguration of the trans-Atlantic service. The Larne Weekly Reporter of 26 April 1873 took a somewhat jaundiced view:

"It is certainly a matter of regret that the new line, inaugurated under the most promising auspices on Saturday, last, between this port and New York, is not in the hands of Irish capitalists. It must be admitted there are plenty of gentlemen to properly float such an undertaking; but we are sorry to say they have neither the spirit nor the enterprise to try the experiment. Still, it must be conceded that, if it were not for some gentlemen whom we have in our midst, such a favour would not be conferred upon us, no matter what natural advantages our seaport might present for transatlantic or other traffic.

"To our friends across the channel, it seems, we are indebted for the boom conferred upon our harbour, who at all times are inclined to invest money in paying speculations. On the present occasion, we believe they have invested to advantage. That the new route will be a complete success we doubt not, but that the entire credit therewith should be given to English, and Scotch capitalists, we do not believe, nor will we coincide with. As was incontestably proved on Saturday last, our harbour is the best suited for the anchorage of such vessels as the Pennsylvania in the North of Ireland, with every convenience at hand for loading and discharging.

"When lying alongside the quay she drew 19 feet water at ebb tide; and she left the harbour, although heavily laden, as if she were in the middle of the Irish Channel – which could be done in few other ports in Ireland by vessels of like dimensions. We have no right to thank our English and Scotch capitalists for this, surely, neither have we any right to thank them for the convenience of our harbour, which have been made at the sole expense of an Irish gentleman, to whom is due, in our opinion, the principal credit of the opening of a new line at the present time.

"If James Chaine Esq had not made the improvements which he has done at the Curran – and to his credit, be it said unassisted – those English and Scotch capitalists of whom we hear so much, would never have thought of favouring our harbour with their ships or ourselves with their company, except for their own aggrandisement.

"If we had a few such men as Mr Chaine in the North of Ireland, things would have been otherwise, as it is, we wish the State Line every success, believing that ultimately the claims of our harbour in this respect must be conceded by even those who have hitherto been against us, and knowing that the town which we represent will be greatly benefited thereby."

The State Line itself was a new commercial venture. According to Ian Duffin: "A few months after the new company called at Larne, the names of these vessels were prefixed 'State of'. This was probably to distinguish them from the Dominion Line ships which were also named after American States. These ships often left Larne with as many as 1,400 souls on board. "Agents were . . . George Pim & Co of Belfast. One of their staff was Mr William McCalla (Billy), who later founded the well-known firm of William McCalla & Co Ltd. He was a well-known figure in Larne on days when State Line ships called. The long line of emigrants would file up the gangway where a Dr Hunter awaited them for their inspection. Sometimes the procession would be halted whilst the doctor made a closer inspection, on the sign of an ailment, which might make an emigrant liable to deportation from America.

"Each emigrant, as is still the law, had to be provided with a contract ticket on which was stated the price of the passage, port of destination, amount of space and scale of provisions to which the passenger was entitled. Men unaccompanied by wives, and single males over 14 years, were usually berthed forward in an open steerage with three beds in each tier. Unmarried and unaccompanied females were berthed aft in similar accommodation."

A framed copy of an advertisement in The Larne Reporter of 9 September, 1882, hangs in the Board Room of the offices of Larne Harbour Ltd, and gives details of the then current rates for the weekly crossing of "one of the full-powered Steam Ships" of the "State Steamship Company", the new name of the State Line. A cabin to New York cost between 12 and 15 guineas, and a return ticket cost from 20-25 guineas. The charge for a Second Cabin was 8 guineas, and the dubious delights of steerage cost 6 guineas. Children under 8 went at half-fare, and for infants less than a year old the cost was a mere guinea.

An advertisement of 9 September 1882 from the Larne Reporter. It gives details of the current rates for the crossing from Larne to New York. A cabin to New York cost from 12–15 guineas, and a return ticket from 20–25 guineas. A framed copy of the advertisement hangs in the boardroom of Larne Harbour Ltd.

There was no charge for medicine or medical attention. A deposit of 5 guineas was required for Cabin Class, or 2 guineas for "Intermediate and Steerage". The advertisement also made it clear that Second Cabin and Steerage passengers would be "forwarded immediately on arrival to Philadelphia, Boston, Baltimore, Portland, Quebec and all other places in the United States and Canada, at lowest rates. Goods discharged and loaded at 42, North River, New York City."

Given the hardships and uncertainties of such a voyage, including rough seas, unsanitary conditions, the lack of fresh provisions and the high probability of illness, there was a great deal of raw courage in the make-up of the people embarking on an adventure which could lead to prosperity in a burgeoning new land but which also would mean, in very many cases, a lifelong severance from family and friends back in Ireland. Not long ago an American writer and military historian, Orr Kelly, called in to the Harbour Office to seek details of the journey of his widowed grandmother who had departed from Larne in 1884 and had travelled steerage with five children to New York. Modern travellers in the age of jet aircraft can hardly begin to visualise such courage and commitment from a young widow who set off alone from Larne with her young brood for a hopefully better life in the New World.

Mr Kelly's wife Mary Davies Kelly, a genealogist, kindly provided the following information about the family's forebears: "The James Kelly family lived in Belfast at 90 Alfred Terrace,

An American writer and military historian Orr Kelly and his wife Mary Davies Kelly, a genealogist, who traced their family forebears in Northern Ireland. Bridget Mary Kelly, a young widow, sailed from Larne in March 1884 with her five young children on the State of Nebraska bound for New York. In the summer of 1998 Orr Kelly called into the Harbour Office to seek details of the journey of his widowed grandmother.

The State of Nebraska, the last State Line vessel to call at Larne, in December 1889.

Castlereagh, where James, the head of the family, was a Coal Merchant. His family consisted of his wife, Bridget Mary, nee O'Connor, and four children: Thomas Joseph, born 15 April 1869; James Francis, born 16 September 1873; Teresa Liguori, born 25 December 1881 and Bridget Mary, born 17 March 1883. When her husband died at the age of 37, on 10 June 1883, Bridget was 8 months pregnant with her fifth child, Charles John, who was born 31 July 1883.

"Family tradition is that the family had planned to emigrate to the United States before James died. Whether his death caused a delay in the travel plans is not known.

"Bridget and her children sailed out of Larne Harbour for the port of New York on the steamship, State of Nebraska, probably between 10 and 14 March 1884. The exact date of sailing is not known, but at that time it usually took a steamship between 10 days and two weeks to make the crossing.

"The ship manifest at the time of the ship's arrival in New York on 24 March 1884 – now on file at the National Archives in Washington DC – shows Passenger Number 97, Mrs Bridget Kelly, age 37, Widow, bound for Boston, 3 bags. The next four passengers listed were her four younger children. Bridget's eldest son, Thomas, was listed separately as Passenger Number 127, Labourer. Thomas may have come aboard the ship later than the rest of the family, or because he had an occupation, was listed separately. All six were in the steerage section of the ship.

"The State of Nebraska was a steam screw ship, built in 1880 by London and Glasgow Shipbuilding Company, and owned by the State Line Steam Ship Company. Her gross tonnage was 3,986 tons and her dimensions were 385 x 43 feet. She had three masts and one funnel. The Nebraska, which entered service in 1880, was one of the newest vessels in the line and was described as 'an ocean greyhound'. The steamship company was established in 1873 and the principal ports were Glasgow and New York. There were eight other ships belonging to the line.

"When Bridget and her family were passengers, the Master of the ship was AG Briar, from Glasgow. There were 423 passengers aboard the vessel, most of them from Scotland and Ireland but others were from Denmark, Russia, Germany, Hungary, Sweden, Norway, England and the United States, according to the ship manifest.

"From New York, the Kelly family went to Boston, where, it is thought, they had either friends or relatives.

"In 1889 the family lived in the company town of Zylonite, new North Adams, Mass. Thomas, the breadwinner of the family, was employed by the American Zylonite Company, which manufactured a forerunner of today's plastics to produce many items that had been made earlier from shell, bone, ivory, hard rubber or metal.

"In January 1891, a New Jersey based company took over the business and shipped all the equipment and machinery to their Pyraline Manufacturing Company in Kearny. The Kelly family, along with a number of former Zylonite employees, followed the move.

"Bridget Kelly died on 5 December 1907 in Arlington, New Jersey.

"The company for which Thomas worked later became the Arlington Company, a subsidiary of El DuPont de Nemours Company. Thomas had become a supervisor by 1905 and in 1931 he retired and with his wife, Catherine, moved to the Hollywood section of Los Angeles near the home of his brother James. He died there on 5 March 1936.

"James, the second son, also worked at the 'celluloid works' for a time. In 1899 he became a lawyer and in 1909 was the youngest judge in the history of Hudson county, New Jersey. In 1913 he moved to California and located in Merced where he was President of the Merced Title Guarantee Company. In 1927 he, Catherine, his wife, and son, James, moved to the Hollywood section of Los Angeles. He was Deputy City Attorney for the city of Los Angeles and died on 3 June 1939.

"Bridget Mary, the eldest daughter, worked for the Arlington Company for a short while. In the early 1920's she became a registered nurse. In 1927 she and her sister, Teresa, had moved to Oakland, California and in 1929 she moved to Hollywood and lived with her brother Thomas. Later she and her sister lived together. She died on 27 June 1955.

"Teresa was a bookkeeper. In 1907 she began her life-long association with the Prudential Life Insurance Company. She worked for them in Hudson county, New Jersey and in Oakland and Los Angeles, California. She and her sister were very close and lived together most of their lives. Teresa died on 5 March 1956.

"Charles also worked for the Arlington Company for a short time. By 1914 he had moved to California and was in Merced, living with his brother, James, and employed as a collector for the San Joaquin Light and Power Company. He was also headquartered in Coalinga and Selma. At the time he enlisted in the US Army, in February 1918, he lived in Selma. He was discharged from the Army in March 1919. In 1920 he and his wife, Edith, moved to San Luis Obispo where Charles became manager of the Midland Counties Public Service Corporation. In 1939 the company was taken over by the Pacific Gas and Electric Company and Charles retained his title until his death, on 2 June 1942. Edith and Charles had two children: Alfred Orr and Charles John."

All of this is a long way from the widow who travelled steerage from Larne to New York in 1884 but it gives a very human dimension to the statistics of 19th Century emigration – and it is a story that could be told, with varying details, many thousands of times over.
The State Line, in its early days at Larne, was fortunate. Ian Duffin notes "At a dinner on board State of Nebraska at Larne in 1883, Mr Chaine, responding to his toast, said that during the ten years State Line had called at Larne, not a bale of goods or a single passenger had been lost. This was probably true as far as passengers from Larne were concerned, but not elsewhere."

Indeed, it was not all plain sailing – in the most literal sense of that term. Ian Duffin, further in his article for the Larne Guardian, recalled several spectacular, and tragic, shipwrecks. "On Christmas Eve morning, 1878, SS State of Louisiana, bound for Larne, stranded on Hunter Rock. There were 30 passengers and 2,000 tons of cargo on board, with a crew of 49. The passengers were taken off, and landed at Larne by tugs which had been rushed from Belfast

to assist. In a short time, there was 15 feet of water in her holds. Some of her cargo was saved, but efforts to keep her afloat were in vain, and she finally broke into three pieces, and sank into deep water. Captain W McGowan was in command.

"At the Board of Trade Inquiry, the master was exonerated, as the defence had no difficulty in proving that the Hunter Rock buoy was about a quarter of a mile away from its proper position, at the time of the casualty. The Belfast News Letter of 13 January 1879, carries a notice of the sale of the wreck. Obviously she cheated any prospective salvers. In 1978, a sub aqua team saw three pieces and the anchors in place on the bows.

"In July 1879, State of Virginia, homeward bound from New York, was stranded on Sable Island and became a total loss. This time there was loss of life – three women and two children. A British gunboat landed the greater part of her crew on the island. A Board of Trade Inquiry was held in Glasgow. As a result, the master's certificate was suspended for three months, but at the end of the period, he was reinstated, this time in command of SS State of Alabama. This master, Captain Moodie often brought a full cargo from New York to Belfast on the ship.

On Christmas Eve morning 1878 the State of Louisiana, bound for Larne, foundered off Hunter Rock. Some of the artefacts brought to the surface many years later included a chamber pot and a glass bottle.

"On one occasion, SS State of Alabama was overdue, and uneasiness was felt for her safety, when a Larne Master, Captain McConnell, commanding 'Humber', one of Dixon's timber ships, arrived and reported he had passed the ship 13 miles west of Tory Island, steering east and all well.

"The worst disaster occurred in 1884, when SS State of Florida was sunk in collision in mid-ocean with the loss of 123 lives, among them Larne and Belfast citizens. She sailed from New York on 12 April and when she was ten days overdue, the sum of 25 guineas per cent was paid for re-insurance. On 7 May, the Donaldson Liner, Titania, arrived at Quebec with 24 survivors of State of Florida, and reported that she had been sunk in collision with the barque Pomona off Chatham. Before being picked up by another sailing ship, the survivors, 44 in number, had been 35 hours in the boats, without food or water. Twenty-four of these survivors had been transferred to Titania.

Another view of the chamber pot in safe hands – from left are Larne men Captain William Close, Jim McCarlie and Tommy Shields.

"The collision occurred on a dark night, and in less than half-an-hour both vessels had foundered, the barque with the loss of all hands except the master and two men. The women on board SS State of Florida refused to board the boats, and only one, a stewardess, was saved. The chief officer, who was in charge of the bridge at the time of the collision, was severely censured, and had his certificate suspended after the Board of Trade Inquiry. The captain, who was drowned (he was on deck a few moments after the collision) was commended for his conduct after he took charge."

On 23 December 1896 the State of Georgia disappeared at sea with the loss of 32 lives, according to Eugene W Smith in his "Trans-Atlantic Passenger Ships Past and Present" (George W Dean Co, Boston, 1947).

Eventually the trans-Atlantic competition became very keen, and in 1890 the State Steamship Company advertised the lowest cabin fares on the Atlantic – 7 to 9 guineas for the crossing, with steerage fares being reduced from 6 to 4 guineas. A contemporary writer noted "owing to some difference of opinion between the directors of the Company and the representatives of the Chaine Estate, these steamers have ceased to call."[11] One wonders what the entrepreneurial James Chaine would have made of it all, had he been alive.

A ship's bell thought to be from a State Line vessel – presented to Larne Harbour Ltd by the family of the late James McClenaghan, a director from 1944 until his death in 1966, and Chairman for 17 years.

Photo: Alf McCreary

The last State Line vessel to call at Larne was the SS State of Nebraska, in December 1889. For some time afterwards there were continued sailings from Glasgow to New York, with calls made in the Foyle. On 4 March 1891, after a special meeting of shareholders in Glasgow, the company went into liquidation. The stirring story of the

The memorial at Curran Park to the many emigrants who left Larne to start a new life in America. The monument, cast in bronze, was designed on the advice of the Ulster-American Committee by sculptor Ed Barton, and was unveiled in May 1992 by Professor Bobby Moss of Blacksburg, South Carolina.

Courtesy of the Northern Ireland Tourist Board

State Line visits to Larne and the many thousands of human stories associated with the emigrants on their way to a hopefully better life in the New World, is commemorated by a simple plaque in the Port Terminal. It states:

> "Erected to the memory of those many emigrants who sailed from this harbour from the 18th Century onwards for a new life in America, including those who voyaged on the ships of the State Line in the 19th century. Their stock provided the United States with Presidents and Pioneers, sturdy and thrifty citizens, and defenders of Liberty."

According to Eugene W Smith (Op.Cit.) there were nine ships in the State Line: "State of Louisiana, built in 1872, 1,869 gross tons; State of Alabama, 1873, 2,313 gross; State of Georgia, 1873, 2,490 gross; State of Pennsylvania, 1873, 2,488 gross; State of Virginia, 1873, 2,472 gross; State of Nevada, 1874, 2,488 gross; State of Indiana, 1874, 2,528 gross; State of Nebraska, 1880, 3,986 gross; and State of Florida, 1881, 4,000 gross.

Though a great deal of income was derived from the passenger trade at Larne, a vast amount of cargo passed through the port each way. "In the 1860s most of the import trade consisted of wheat for the flour mills. Much of this was from foreign ports although some came from

Liverpool in small schooners. In 1868 at least twelve foreign ships brought wheat for Macauley's flour mills and in 1873 imports of grain amounted to 12,000 tons.

"Iron ore, mined at Kilwaughter from 1867, was transported by cart to the 'Curran Wharves' for export. Carters were paid at the rate of 2 shillings per ton for the removal of the ore from the mines to 'Mr Service's Quay'. This was not a very satisfactory arrangement as the mine owners were dependent mainly on local farmers and their horses which were not available on a regular basis. Initially it was mentioned that 'should the mines prove productive in point of quantity and quality, the necessity of laying a tramway from Kilwaughter to the quays might soon suggest itself.' . . . In the 1880s the main exports from the harbour were cattle, bauxite, iron ore, paper, flour, pork, butter, oatmeal, potatoes and linen. Imports were raw flax, coal, wheat, Indian corn, timber and general merchandise. Imports of coal increased rapidly over the period being studied – this can be explained by the increasing domestic and industrial use of the fuel. Much of this coal was unloaded at the Bank Quays in the earlier years, and only 22 colliers carrying 2,500 tons were discharged at Larne Harbour in 1873. Coal vessels, on their return trips, sometimes carried oats, beans, lime or limestone."[12]

On the Ballymena-Larne railway line the main cargo from Larne was coal, and also large quantities of esparto grass and wood pulp for Ballyclare Paper Mill. On the inward trip to Larne large quantities of iron ore were carried for transport to England. By 1882 the tonnage of almost 76,000 was the largest in the line's history but three years later this had dropped to 65,800, due to a decrease in English demand. The number of passengers also decreased and in 1889, the line was sold to the Belfast and Northern Counties Railway. A year later the company amalgamated with the Carrickfergus and Larne railway.

"In 1890 the C&L Railway successfully negotiated terms for amalgamation with the B&NC. In this case the Company was in a much more prosperous position than the Ballymena – Larne Company and the terms of sale were 'stock for stock'. In the same year, a new station, designed by Wise and costing £3,000, was erected at the Harbour. It consisted of two district portions separated by a road. The gap was bridged by a level-crossing, the gates of which incorporated platform sections, thus the closed gates created a continuous platform. The double-faced platform served the broad gauge on one side and the narrow gauge on the other. The large clock on the concourse had two minute hands to show both English and Irish time, the latter being 25 minutes later than Greenwich Mean Time. In this period Irish time was used by all Irish railways."[13]

Just four years prior to the new century, there was a dramatic development which could have had fundamental repercussions for the future of Larne Harbour. The story is told by Jane Ludlow: "In 1896 the authorities in charge of the port of Larne offered to sell their entire rights in the port and harbour for the sum of £90,000, (the average income of the harbour was £4,000), to the Belfast Harbour Commissioners. At the August meeting of the Harbour Commissioners the Chairman, Mr James Musgrave, suggested that it would be in the interests of Belfast to make the purchase. He argued that if Larne 'got into the hands of a syndicate with a railway company . . . it might be worked in such a way as to carry past Belfast altogether a large proportion of the trade that now passed through the hands of

Belfast.' One of the Commissioners, Sir Daniel Dixon, himself a native of Larne, opposed the purchase on the grounds that 'the people of Larne had pushed the Harbour as far as possible' and there would be little increase in revenue. Musgrave considered that the matter should be postponed until the Belfast Harbour Engineer had made his report and no positive action was taken at that time.

"At least one Larne resident, Donald Macdonald, thought that the port would benefit from the sale – Macdonald had been the engineer for the construction of the Harbour in the 1860s and in 1896 was Harbour Engineer and Manager. He put forward the idea that by constructing a graving dock at Larne the congestion in the repair yards at Belfast would be eased. The dock would help develop a great industry the nucleus of which was already established at the Olderfleet Shipyard."[14]

It is interesting to note, however, that Donald Macdonald, to whom James Chaine had entrusted, with his son William, the future of Larne Harbour, was prepared to contemplate the sale of the port. As Harbour Engineer and Manager in 1896 he would have been in a key position to make a sound commercial judgement on such a deal, but the decision was postponed by the Belfast Harbour Commissioners, and the moment was lost. The Larne Harbour Co survived, and with a not inconsiderable record of achievement in the previous decades, turned to face the rigours, and the opportunities, of the new century.

---

1.   References to James Chaine's Will are extracted from the Probate and Matrimonial Division of the High Court of Justice, Ireland, in the District Registry of Belfast 1885.
2.   Ibid.
3.   Jane M Ludlow BSc, Op.Cit. p65.
4.   Op.Cit. Fraser G. McHaffie, pp85-86.
5.   Ibid, p91.
6.   Ibid, p89.
7.   Ibid, pp92 and 95.
8.   Larne Harbour Ltd Minute Book PRONI D 1326/32/58.
9.   Op.Cit. Jane M Ludlow, p66.
10.   Ibid, p67.
11.   Ibid, p67.
12.   Ibid, p67-68.
13.   Ibid, pp70-71.
14.   Ibid, p71.

S.S. NEVADA AT LARNE. RW.270.

A Robert Welch picture of the Liner State of Nevada, a vessel of 2,488 tons gross, built in 1874, and one of the nine ships of the State Line which provided a trans-Atlantic service from Larne.

This fine view of the Port of Larne in 1872 by James Valentine shows Larne shipyard (foreground) with the harbour and sailing ships in the background.

J.V. 16736

CHAPTER 4

THE GATHERING STORM

The early years of the new century set the tone for one of the most dynamic and also one of the bloodiest centuries in the history of mankind. Some 1,500 Europeans were massacred in the Boxer uprising in China, and the Boer War dragged on, while in individual acts of anarchy the Italian King was shot dead in Monza, and the Prince of Wales survived a murder attempt in Brussels. Ominously, the German Reichstag announced further naval expansion, and the world's biggest battleship, the Mikasa, was launched at Barrow-in-Furness for the Japanese Government.

On the artistic scene, Mrs Lillie Langtry "wowed" Washington, and Oscar Wilde died in disgrace in Paris. In the world of sport Jim Jeffries of the United States won the World Heavyweight Boxing Championship by knocking out the former holder James J Corbett in the 23rd round, and at tennis, America won the first Davis Cup. The new fashions dictated that women's' hemlines were getting shorter, just a little, and in 1900 Coca-Cola arrived in Britain some 14 years after its introduction to the United States.

A major historical development of the new century was the death of Queen Victoria in January 1901 at the age of 81. She had reigned for 63 years, a period which witnessed the remarkable expansion of British interests worldwide, and of industrial transformation at home. Her death marked not only the end of an era, but the beginning of a new world order in the 20th century, characterised by the increasing affluence of the developed world and a descent into the mass violence of two World Wars, as well as recurring gangsterism and terrorism.

This is a splendid study by W. Lawrence of the Princess Beatrice on the Larne–Stranraer service. She was a 550-ton paddle-steamer built by Harland and Wolff, and worked the route from 1875 to 1904, taking 2^1/$_2$ hours for the crossing.

Courtesy of the National Library of Ireland C2341

It was against this chequered world background that the port of Larne developed steadily as a successful commercial undertaking which maintained the physical link with Britain, but it, too, was to

play its part not only in the prosperity but also in the violent upheavals of the 20th century. Larne Harbour Ltd, which had existed since 1891, was reconstituted as the so-called "New Company" early in the century, while the port itself played a major role in the two World Wars and, in the North of Ireland, during the Home Rule Crisis.

Commercially, the link with Stranraer continued to prosper, and provided a regular and mostly reliable link between the two islands. In 1901 a marine survey of the Princess Victoria and the Princess

Another view of the Princess Beatrice alongside the quay at Larne. Two gangways are in position for boarding. The general facilities for passengers are poor.

May indicated that each had only three further years as a suitable vessel for the route, and that major repairs would be necessary to prolong their usefulness. The reserve steamer, the Princess Beatrice, was regarded as 'quite inadequate'. In 1903 an order was placed with William Denny and Bros Ltd to build a turbine-driven vessel, at a cost of £66,000 and on 1 June 1904, the Princess Maud – built at a cost of £600 more than the estimate – took over the mail service at Stranraer. She was the first turbine steamer on the Irish Sea, and initially knocked ten minutes off the time taken by the paddle vessels. The Princess May was then based in Larne for the summer daylight service, the Princess Victoria became the reserve ship, and the old Princess Beatrice was sold for breaking up.[1]

The Princess Maud had accommodation to match her upgraded performance on the crossing. "Princess Maud had two covered decks and the promenade and boat decks. The boat deck extended to the side of the steamer and this provided shelter for the promenade deck below. Aft on the promenade deck was to be found the ladies' lounge for steerage passengers, while below that was a combined lounge and tea-room and below that again a general steerage lounge. As became the tradition for so many years, all the steerage accommodation was situated aft of the after hatch and connected with the rest of the ship by a hinged gangway. (In the previous Stranraer ships the steerage accommodation had been for'ard.) Most of the first-class accommodation on the promenade deck was devoted to four staterooms plus dormitory-style sleeping accommodation for twenty-five. There was also a ladies' cabin and the first-class bar. On the main deck there was situated a dining saloon with seating for sixty-four, while the balance of the space on this deck was occupied by staterooms and officers' accommodation. The crew's quarters were forward on this deck and on the deck below."[2]

The Princess Maud, like her predecessors, encountered storm damage and serious operational mishaps. On 6 August 1909 during fog in Loch Ryan, she sliced into the anchored cargo ship Pirate which sank within ten minutes. Four passengers from the Pirate managed to climb up a rope ladder to the Maud, including one female who was in bad health. Some

of the Pirate's crew managed to escape in one of the lifeboats, taking with them the lady's cat, which was more fortunate than her owner, who later died. The rest of the Pirate's crew managed to climb aboard the Maud.[3]

In April 1912, a new Princess Victoria, another turbine-driven vessel, took over the mail route, the former Princess Victoria having been sold in February 1910. "Maiden voyages are usually festive occasions, but not this one. Two weeks previously the White Star liner Titanic sank while on her first voyage, and this cast a gloom over the maiden trip by Princess Victoria. One lady refused to board the ship on Monday morning when she learnt that this was to be a maiden voyage. A more lasting result of the Titanic disaster was the tightening up of lifeboat requirements. In 1913 both turbine steamers were fitted with an additional lifeboat, buoyant deck seats were added, and two cutters on each ship were converted into lifeboats. (During overhaul in the spring of 1907 two lifeboats had been removed from the after deck of Princess Maud.)[4]

Meanwhile, commercially, the Larne Harbour Company made steady progress under the direction of William Chaine and Donald MacDonald. The charges for the use of the harbour covered just about anything that moved through the port – the "rates to be levied on goods and merchandise at the harbour, pier, quays and landing places" included everything from aerated waters and alum cake, to bran, brandy, cattle, chalk, cotton, cotton-seed cake, divi divi, drugs, lard, kerbstones, lorries, common manure, sugar, vitriol, waste, whiting, whisky, wild animals, and much, much more! The list itself gives some indication of the huge diversity of cargoes carried and unloaded.[5] The range of vessels covered in the same list also gives a clear picture of the types of vessels using the harbour in the latter part of the 19th century – passenger steamers, pleasure boats, steam tugs and steamboats, barques, brigs, schooners and smacks.

William Chaine, Donald MacDonald and a Thomas Jack from Glasgow were founder-members of the Shamrock Shipping Co Ltd, which was formed in 1897 by the merger of six single-ship companies, namely The Argus, Curran, Rochefort, North Devon, Larne and Shamrock

Steamship Companies Ltd. Six steamships were delivered within six years – the Raloo (1898), the Clonlee (1899), the sister-ships Glynn (1899) and Curran (1900), the Gransha (1901) and the Skeldon (1903). For almost 80 years, the company and its vessels made a distinctive contribution to seafaring worldwide. It was taken over in 1976 by Dorman Shipping Ltd. (A detailed account of the Shamrock Shipping vessels and of their service dates and ultimate disposal was printed in the magazine Sea Breezes, Vol 50, No 372 in December 1976.)

In the early part of the new century, Donald MacDonald retired after long and faithful service at the Harbour. He married a young Scottish woman, and went to live at Lockerbie, near Dumfries, having taken over several Larne Harbour craftsmen to build his new house. The retirement of MacDonald was thought to have been one of the deciding factors which made William Chaine dispose of the "Old Company".[6] The new company was bought by a group of local businessmen, principally Charles MacKean who was Chairman until his death in 1943, and others including Sir William Brown, JJ Kirkpatrick and WJR Harbinson.

The first meeting was held at the Company's Registered Offices on 31 July 1912. Those present included the above-mentioned Directors, plus another Director James Sutherland, with the company solicitor JW McNinch and Company Secretary J Agnew "in attendance". Mr Agnew was to be paid a salary of £250 per annum. It was decided that the Belfast Banking Company Ltd be appointed as bankers, Messrs Ashworth Mosley and Co as auditors, and that three Directors should form a quorum. The nominal capital of the Company was £65,000 in £10 shares , and the major shareholders were JJ Kirkpatrick (£15,000), WN and CJ Brown (£15,000), the MacKean family (£11,000) and WJR Harbinson (£3,500). CL MacKean andWJR Harbinson , trading as Howden Brothers, jointly held shares worth £10,000.[7] Business was brisk, though mundane. The topics included the purchase of a four-ton electric crane (deferred), the inadequate supply of railway wagons, and machines for screening coal.[8] At the next meeting, on 28 August 1912, there was a slightly more contentious matter. Shipowners were objecting to a proposal to charge an extra two shillings per 100 tons be charged to all vessels, to cover the cost of insurance. The Board decided to postpone further consideration until a special meeting when all members would be present.

The minutes of the Board Meetings over the next couple of years show a picture of a prospering port, with Directors turning their attention to such varied issues as iron ore exports, tenders for coal tubs, the purchase of cranes, the supply of railway wagons, and business dealings with the British Aluminium Co. Ltd.

This factory which converted locally-mined bauxite into pure alumina was opened on Christmas Day 1895, when almost 100 men started work. Though it was known as the Aluminium Works, no aluminium was refined in Larne. The alumina was shipped to a plant near Inverness where the aluminium was produced. There was a 3ft gauge railway connecting the works to the Harbour, and this transported the minerals and coal, which was shipped from Greenock in the Company's own vessel. One of the small locomotives was later preserved, and was used on the Shane's Castle Railway in Co Antrim. The waste product from the Larne plant, mainly red iron oxide, was dumped in large ponds on the foreshore, known as the Sloblands – access to which was by a long siding which passed over the broad and the narrow-gauge

E. J. Featherstone

Andrew Ferguson.

Larne Harbour Factory.

Harold Martin

R. Mc F. Giffen.

The British Aluminium Co. Ltd. which converted locally-mined bauxite into pure alumina, opened on Christmas Day 1895. It provided steady employment for Larne until its closure in 1947. This water-colour sketch was part of an elaborate book of drawings presented to the manager, James Sutherland, on his retirement.

railway lines. The plant was initially a great success, with double shifts quickly established, and more and more workers employed.

Labour relations, however, were not always trouble – free, and the Larne Weekly Telegraph of 14 June 1913 reported a sudden and dramatic deterioration. "On the evening of the 4th inst a strike was declared amongst the labourers employed at the British Aluminium Company's works at Larne Harbour. Ostensibly the object of the strike was to obtain shorter hours and better working conditions, but during the past week it has become apparent that the real point at issue is the recognition of the Irish Transport Worker's Union, whose officials have been at work organising the men for some time past.

"Shortly before the night shift was due to start on the 4th inst the union officials requested an interview with the manager (Mr James Sutherland) to discuss certain grievances. The consultation did not prove satisfactory, and the delegates directed the night men not to commence work, the day men acquiescing in that decision. As a consequence the workers are at a standstill as far as the ordinary processes are concerned, only a few mechanics being still engaged in repairs, overhauling machinery, and etc.

"Mass meetings of the men have been held almost each day, and on Wednesday and Thursday last a great many of them joined the trades union mentioned above. The strike affects about 350 men, and, it is almost needless to say, the shopkeepers of the town view the prospect with dismay, as it must mean the loss of at least £500 a week to the town.
"The management assert the officials of the union have treated them in a very high-handed manner, as whilst they have always been willing to listen to and redress grievances, on this

occasion no demands were formulated. On being asked for an interview the manager stated that he must have time to consult his directors, which would take a couple of days. Such a delay was refused, and a strike was declared at a few minutes' notice. Interviewed yesterday (the 11th inst), Mr Sutherland reiterated that he was perfectly willing to discuss with the men any grievances, they alleged, as heretofore, but that his directors would not in any way recognise the union. Thus the issue is clearly joined, and it remains with the men to decide whether the recognition of the union is at all a vital matter to them.

"That the men may have grievances is not unlikely, but in the face of the assertion that the management are ready and willing to negotiate and make concessions, the feeling is growing that the strike is an ill-advised action on the part of the union officials."

There was, however, a happy ending which may have been partly due to a little Divine intervention, as the next week's Larne Weekly Telegraph reported: "To the gratification of the people of Larne the industrial strike at the British Aluminium Company's Works came to an end on Tuesday morning, when the men, with few exceptions resumed work after a conference with the manager on the previous day. In bringing about peace the clergymen of the town can claim a great deal of the credit, having on Sunday last discussed matters with the members of their congregations who are employed at the Aluminium Works. At their joint request Mr Sutherland received on Monday a deputation of men representing different departments of the industry, and as a consequence peace was declared that evening despite the rigorous protests of the trades union's officials supposed to be conducting the strike.

"The grievances alleged by the men were excess of working hours and insufficient wages, and it is understood that the manager, Mr James Sutherland, has made considerable concessions in both respects. On the other hand, the management declare that they were always willing to consider and redress grievances, but declined under any circumstances to recognise the authority of the Irish Transport Workers' Union, some of whose officials had been organising the men, and who declared the strike at a few minutes' notice.

"Under all the circumstances the terms of settlement mutually arranged between the men and the management are distinctly honourable. The men secure better working conditions, and the management have vindicated their stand against the recognition of the union. Needless to say, the shopkeepers of the town are delighted at the early resumption of work . . ." No doubt they felt that the exhortations of the town's clergy had borne fruit, and that good business was next to godliness!

At its peak, the plant employed 400-500 people, and was one of the economic mainstays of the town, but the discovery of richer bauxite deposits in France and elsewhere, plus the commercial need to site an alumina plant nearer coalfields to reduce transport costs, led to the closure of the Larne plant in the middle of the 20th century. This economic loss was offset to some extent, however, by the development of the harbour which in turn utilised what was left by the reclamation of the Sloblands, to expand further. All of this, however, was a long way from the grim reality of the First World War which broke out some two decades after the British Aluminium Company was established.

It was not until August 1914 that the Minutes of the Larne Harbour Co Ltd gave the first indication of the impending cataclysm of the First World War, when the Board discussed payment to the families of harbour employees who had volunteered or had been called up for military service. The Directors decided, as the wives of these men were to benefit from the Prince of Wales Fund, that instead of direct assistance, a contribution of £50 be given to the fund.

However, the requests for direct help continued, and in an apparent change of policy, the Company decided at the Board meeting of September 1914 to pay 10 shillings a week each to the wives and families of two married men, and to consider the case of a third man who was said to have been "the principal support of his mother." It was decided at the next Board Meeting on 28 October 1914 to give her five shillings weekly "in the meantime".[9]

There was no mention in the Minutes, however, of one of the most historic and controversial events in the history of Larne Harbour – namely, the gun-running episode of 24 April 1914. That night a small coal-boat The Clyde Valley sailed into Larne Lough with a consignment of around 26,000 weapons and some 3 million rounds of ammunition to arm the Ulster Unionists in their defiance of Home Rule for Ireland.

The story itself had elements of high drama and more than a whiff of skulduggery and subterfuge. Major Fred Crawford, a leading Unionist, bought the SS Fanny in Bergen, with the full knowledge of the leadership, to transport the weapons and ammunition, which he had bought from a Hamburg dealer, across the Baltic to the Irish Sea. The cargo was transferred in Danish territorial waters, and the authorities became suspicious. However the Fanny slipped into the Baltic mists and began her journey. The British authorities had more than an inkling of impending trouble, and to confuse them, it was decided to purchase another vessel to complete the voyage to Larne.

The Clyde Valley, often seen in Belfast Lough and therefore more liable to avoid suspicion, was purchased for £4,500 in Glasgow. The Clyde Valley drew alongside the Fanny off Tuskar Rock, where the arms and ammunition were exchanged. Subsequently, The Balmerino , another Ulster coal boat, made for Belfast Lough as a decoy, while the Clyde Valley (named Mountjoy II after the vessel which broke the boom in the 17th century Seige of Derry) sailed into Larne Harbour around 10.30 pm. Crawford noted later "The harbour was brilliantly lighted – number two hold was opened and the arms were landed on the wharf. As each crane load was landed, a motor car came along quietly, gathered as many bundles as it could hold, and then drove off rapidly in the darkness to its destination."

Earlier that day, the Ulster Volunteer Force, set up by the Ulster Unionist Council in 1913, issued "An Important Notice – Mobilise tonight at Market Yard at 7.30 pm sharp bringing overcoat, food for a few hours and stout stick." The Notice added, ironically "No firearms". From the early afternoon on 24 April, cars from various parts had been converging on Larne Harbour. By mid-evening Larne and the main access routes to the town had been sealed off by local Volunteers. The police discovered, too late, that it had been more than yet another mobilisation exercise! (The historian David Fitzpatrick claims, however, that the arms and ammunition were landed "with police connivance".)[10]

By 11.00 pm cranes were unloading the cargo and the arms were transported by car all over the Province. Some were brought back to nearby Magheramorne by horse-drawn carts! A special correspondent for the Larne Times and Weekly Telegraph noted: "It was quite a moving spectacle at the quay some hundred yards from the Olderfleet Hotel, when the quiet April midnight was turned into the busy scene of day, full of life and stir, the hum of the donkey engine of the good ship Mountjoy echoing to the 'konk kink' of the motors as they cleared off with their valuable cargoes."

Home Rule Crisis – a cutting from the 'Belfast Evening Telegraph' of 25 April 1914 records the sense of astonishment at the gun-running episode.

Weapons and ammunition were also unloaded to the Innismurray for transportation to Donaghadee, and the Roma, bound for Belfast. The Clyde Valley, or Mountjoy II, once her Larne consignment had been unloaded, set sail for Bangor with supplies for local Volunteers. It had been a remarkably smooth – and highly illegal – operation, with the only casualties being a coast guard who died of a heart attack, a driver whose car ran into the back of another vehicle, and a crew member of the Clyde Valley who fell into the hold.

Dr David Hume, in his account of the gun-running "For Ulster and Her Freedom" (published by the Ulster Society) states "In history, it is often simple actions which make the strongest statements; the sight of ordinary farmers coming home from Larne, in the early hours, their carts laden with guns from the Mountjoy, says much about the commitment of the unionist community at every level. In another simple action, Fred Crawford painted three strips of canvas with the word 'Mountjoy' to re-name the Clyde Valley and symbolise his belief that he was taking part in another relief operation. These were simple actions, but the statements which they conveyed were powerful in themselves."

In 1968 an aged Clyde Valley was brought back from Canada, but amid acrimony she received insufficient financial support and had to be towed away to an ignominious end.

In 1964, on the 50th Anniversary of the gun-running episode, a plaque was unveiled at Chaine Memorial Road, within sight of the Chaine Tower by the then Unionist Prime Minister Captain Terence O'Neill. (The memorial was originally situated in front of the Olderfleet Hotel and then relocated when the road was widened.) It was mounted on a large stone plinth with, on the top, the lamp which had guided the vessel into Larne on that historic night. Inside the memorial was one of the original rifles, and copies of the Belfast Telegraph and the East Antrim Times.

With hindsight, the gun-running was a remarkable episode which took place at the start of a violent century during which the upheavals on the island of Ireland led to fundamental changes in both North and South. One or other side in this ancient quarrel tends to have a selective

The Unionist opposition to Home Rule is clearly illustrated by this picture of the workers at Larne Foundry circa 1914. The young man in the front row, fourth from the left, is David Logan, who later was a successful and popular manager of the Port.

Picture courtesy of Miss Isabelle Logan

memory about the use and legitimacy of violence, but events at Larne in 1914 and in Dublin two years later, showed that no side had a prerogative of innocence. Clearly very few people were aware in advance of the gun-running into Larne, but there was no doubt that William Chaine was very much party to what was going on. The historian Dr ATQ Stewart notes in his book "The Ulster Crisis", published originally by Faber and Faber: "Chaine, the commander of the 2nd Battalion of the Central Antrim UVF, was chairman of the company which owned the harbour and was therefore able to make the arrangements." Chaine, in fact, was not Chairman of the Board, but he had used his contacts to make out a detailed intelligence report on Harbour employees and others. This was not an activity which was likely to be discussed at the next Board Meeting!

When the First World War began in August 1914, amid scenes of euphoria in London where many people thought it would be all over by Christmas, the port of Larne immediately became strategically important for embarking and disembarking troops and supplies, and as a naval base. There had been a naval training establishment at Curran Point in the late 19th century, and references to this were contained in the Larne Times and Weekly Telegraph of 3 June and 22 June 1893. A battery had been erected in 1865 but, according to the newspaper a decision was taken to provide a new battery at a cost of £1,507. (A fuller account is outlined by Captain W Close in "The Corran", Vol 3 No 8.)

In 1914 the decision was taken to sell off the last Stranraer paddle steamer, and the Princess May set off for Swansea on 10 December. It was planned to provide a third turbine vessel for the route, but due to the outbreak of the War, no replacement was made. The Princess Victoria was taken over by the Government for war duties, and she left for the South Coast of England where she spent the next five years in war service. The Princess May spent the war as an accommodation ship in the Orkneys, and was sold in 1920 by the Admiralty for scrap. The third vessel, the Princess Maud was left to maintain the Larne-Stranraer link on her own, and she was later equipped with a machine gun and smoke apparatus due to the threat from German submarines.[11]

At the November Board meeting of 1914, the directors were informed that the Liverpool steamer had been withdrawn without notice due to the danger of floating mines, but the Larne-Stranraer service was maintained throughout the war. "Sailings had to be frequently made at irregular times, based on the latest reports of submarines. Sailings usually took place by the peacetime route, though on occasions deviations were necessary. An escort consisting of two destroyers and a small airship was provided. The Larne steamer loaded with troops would have been a good kill for any submarine. Later in the war when the British Navy was based in Lough Swilly, large numbers of navy men passed through Larne, coming from or rejoining ships.[12]

The Olderfleet Hotel became a naval headquarters. "A wireless mast was erected there, and another at Sandy Bay, two of the first direction – finding installations in the United Kingdom. Among the naval auxiliary ships was the Holyhead to Kingstown mail steamer Tara, which later went to the Mediterranean and was sunk by a submarine. The survivors many of whom were Larne men, were landed in North Africa.

"The officers and men who manned the ships at Larne were at first drawn chiefly from the Royal Naval Reserve. These were however transferred to other parts and replaced by newly-trained men. Many of the sailors who came to Larne were drawn from a training centre near the Crystal Palace.

"Captain, later Admiral Carpendale, was in command of the Larne Naval base during part of the War, and handled the anti submarine campaign with great efficiency."[13]

The geographical situation of Larne made it a particularly good anti-submarine base. "The old battleship Thetis was stationed for a time at Larne, but was later withdrawn and used as a blockship in the attack on Zeebrugge. There were also trawlers from Hull, Grimsby, Yarmouth, Fleetwood, Lowestoft, Aberdeen, Stornoway, and other fishing ports. Hastily armed and equipped they were sent to patrol the northern approaches. About two hundred of these trawlers were based at Larne, and their main function was the maintenance of the anti-submarine nets between Rathlin and the Scottish mainland and at other points in the channel. The guns with which these trawlers were armed were inadequate both in weight of metal and range to offer any serious resistance to the submarines. Gun crews however had their successes, and a trawler commanded by a Lieutenant Peat, sank a submarine in a running battle off Rathlin Island, and brought several survivors to Larne. When trawlers

His Majesty's drifter Moylan on slipways at Larne Shipbuilding & Repair Co., Curran Point. The wooden vessel had her engines removed for overhaul and the hull is being caulked with oakum and pitch. This vessel is probably being reconditioned prior to handing back to her owners at the end of the Great War. The variety of tools on display indicates the range of trades of the local work force.

became equipped with depth charges they were in a much better position to attack, and had a decided advantage over the submarine."[14]

The Board Minutes of Larne Harbour Ltd testify to another battle, in this case a running battle with the Admiralty about the cost of providing a base and supplies for the war effort. The Minutes of 24 February 1915 give the background.

"Some correspondence with the Admiralty was read. One of the letters had reference to stronger measures being necessary to protect the shipping of these coasts against the enemies' submarines, to which the Admiralty replied that this matter had received and was receiving the special attention of the Lords Commissioners of the Admiralty.

"The other letter had reference to the danger of attack on Harbour Property by the Enemy, owing to the place being used by the Admiralty as a Naval Base and asking whether if the Property should suffer damage under such circumstances, the Admiralty would indemnify this Company against all loss arising therefrom to which an acknowledgement, stating the matter will receive attention, has been received."[15] The Admiralty replied, somewhat cannily, that "each case of damage to Property would be separately considered on its merits."

There was also a long correspondence and dispute with the Admiralty about the supply of fresh water at Larne for naval vessels, and as late as 1918, this was still a matter of contention. The Minutes of the Board meeting of 25 November stated "No reply had been received from either the Commodore or the Admiralty to our letter re charge for water supply to Admiralty ships."[16]

Despite the bloody and stirring events of the First World War which cost so many lives and which marked the end of a kind of comparative European innocence – given the degree of slaughter during the rest of the century – there is little or no mention in the Board Minutes of the conflict after July 1916. The main business continued to be the inspection of livestock, details of cattlepens and cranes, and associated matters.

Hidden between the lines, however, were some human stories which reflected upon the social mores of the times. In September 1914, the Board was informed that a Mr D Thompson had resigned from the office staff and as it was thought there might be some difficulty in getting a suitable male successor "it was decided to try a girl". The Company Secretary was asked to approach a Miss Doag "at present employed by the Sun Laundry at 10 shillings weekly" and if "she was considered satisfactory, to offer her £36 per annum to start with". Despite the Directors' trepidation at the thought of replacing a male by "trying" a girl, Miss Doag accepted the post and by the end of 1917 her salary had increased to £52 per annum. By comparison the Company Secretary was being paid £400 a year.[17]

Incidentally, an unnamed office boy who had been employed "on trial" in October 1914, the month Miss Doag started with the Company, also made satisfactory progress and by November 1918, his salary had risen to £12 per annum.

Whatever the upheavals that had convulsed Europe during the same period, and the inestimable suffering of millions of people as a new world order was painfully shaped, at least two Larne Harbour employees had cause to look back with satisfaction – Miss Doag and the unnamed office boy both had had a good war!

ABOVE: Studies of early Larne by James Valentine, circa 1918. The picture shows the sea reaching almost to the Olderfleet Road, with assorted boats and ladies on the beach with their parasols. In the centre background is the railway station, between the quay on the right and the Olderfleet Hotel. J.V. 15998

RIGHT: The Laharna Hotel, and a jaunting car. This is part of a set of Valentine portraits around the end of World War I. J.V. 31136

A Valentine view of Curran Road, on the approach to the harbour. The church-like building in the centre was the former Olderfleet Public Elementary School, since demolished. The writer Amanda McKettrick Ros lived in a house near the site. Her husband Andrew was at one time station-master at Larne. J.V. 20058

A photograph of Larne Harbour Flute Band in 1891, posing outside the "State Line" Hotel.

1. Op.Cit. Fraser G MacHaffie, pp99-101.
2. Ibid. p100.
3. Ibid. p102.
4. Ibid. p104.
5. Harbour Rates for Curran (Larne) 1888, printed by Archer and Sons, Wellington Place, Belfast.
6. PRONI D1570/1.
7. PRONI D3947/A/1 pp1-4.
8. Op.Cit. pp4-5.
9. Op.Cit. pp80-84.
10. The Oxford Illustrated History of Ireland, edited by Professor Roy Foster, p231 (published by the Oxford University Press 1989).
11. Op.Cit. Fraser G MacHaffie, pp104-108.
12. Chronological Events at Larne Harbour, p1 (Documents in possession of Larne Harbour Ltd).
13. Ibid. p3.
14. Ibid. p2.
15. PRONI D3947/A/1 p100.
16. PRONI D3947/A/2 p30.
17. PRONI D3947/A/1 pp83 and 218.

The "Lull", believed to be the tender for the Argenta prison ship, circa 1924.

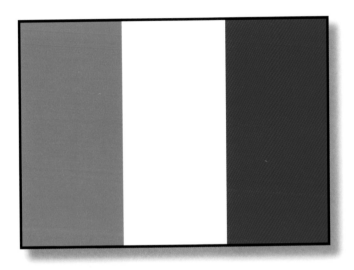

CHAPTER 5

BETWEEN THE WARS

n the aftermath of the First World War, the nations of Europe began to pick up the pieces after that bitter conflict, which claimed more than 10 million lives, but there was unfinished business in Ireland which affected every aspect of life on the island. The contrast between the emergence of a new global order, and the unchanged realities of the vicious Irish conflict was summarised memorably by Winston Churchill:

"Then came the Great War. Every institution, almost, in the world was strained. Great Empires have been overturned. The whole map of Europe has been changed. The position of countries has been violently altered. The modes of thought of men, the whole outlook on affairs, the grouping of parties, all have encountered violent and tremendous changes in the deluge of the world. But as the deluge subsides and the waters fall short we see the dreary steeples of Fermanagh and Tyrone emerging once again. The integrity of their quarrel is one of the few institutions that has been unaltered in the cataclysm which has swept the world."

The integrity of that quarrel had an adverse effect on trade at Larne Harbour. The upheavals in Ireland culminated in the War of Independence and the partition of the island, with the resultant formation of the Irish Free State and of Northern Ireland. This created uncertainty and unrest which led to a sharp decrease in traffic between Scotland and Ireland.

In addition, industrial unrest created more disruption on the Larne-Stranraer link than had taken place during the First World War, and the General Strike of 1926 created its own problems, including a decreased service between Northern Ireland and Scotland. In the latter half of the Twenties, however, sea traffic began to build up, and despite the depression of the Thirties there was, ironically, a boom in coastal shipping.

This early 1920's view from Islandmagee shows the Princess Maud alongside the quay. To the left of the funnels is the Olderfleet Hotel.

The minutes of Larne Harbour Ltd during the inter-war period paint a picture of a company surviving during hard times, and of expanding its facilities within the financial and other resources

available. There was an attempt to foster the development of a fish-processing business at Larne, which ended in failure and in acrimonious legal wrangling. Attempts were made to create new outlets, where possible, and to encourage new tenants. However, cut-backs in wages, including a temporary withdrawal of a long-established annual gratuity, underlined the difficulties facing the workers, at a time when economic conditions were harsh and summary dismissals were not uncommon.

By the end of the Thirties, however, the Company was in a better position to expand, and the creation of the first proper loading ramps for motorised vehicles gave a hint of the way forward. However, the Board was wary about the possibilities of success in this field and asked for guarantees for compensation if the venture did not prove successful! Sadly, however, the shadow of the First World War, with its potential for the renewal of global conflict, hung over these years. And yet this conflict in itself led to unforeseen developments which would ensure the future prosperity of the port.

A Clyde 'Puffer' arriving at Larne, around 1924, with an open bridge from which the crew operated in all weathers.

By the end of 1919, the Princess Victoria, which had undertaken war service on the coast of Southern England, was released by the Admiralty, and after some £62,000 had been spent on re-furbishing, she arrived back for duty at Stranraer on 22 April 1920. The Princess Maud, which had maintained the Larne-Stranraer link during the war, then underwent a £5,000 overhaul.

The endemic disorder in Ireland and continued industrial unrest brought the Larne-Stranraer route to a low ebb. The route was closed from 29 September to 4 October 1919 due to a rail strike, and a coal strike the next year led to the service being suspended for five days. In 1921, when the coal crisis continued, the Government ordered the withdrawal of the service from 15 April to 11 July. During this enforced suspension of the link, the old rivalry from the Donaghadee-Portpatrick route re-emerged, but this opportunistic competition ceased when the Larne-Stranraer service re-started.[1]

By 1923, there was evidence of new stirrings. All the constituent companies of the Larne and Stranraer Steamship Joint Committee were absorbed into the London Midland and Scottish Railway, following the passing of the Railways Act two years earlier. One of the most visible signs of the new changes was the disappearance of the old flag containing the Red Hand of Ulster, and the emergence of a new company flag with a red St George's Cross and in the centre the symbols of the three constituent countries – a rose, a thistle and a harp.[2] On 4 June 1923, the Princess Victoria resumed her mail run, and later that summer the daylight service between Larne and Stranraer was re-established.

Meanwhile, the Board of Larne Harbour Ltd busied itself with re-adjusting to the challenges of post-war business. On 22 January 1919, the Chairman Mr CL MacKean asked for more information about the Agreement between his company and the Larne and Stranraer Steamship Joint Committee. He also suggested a meeting with the Secretary of the Joint Committee "to discuss the present state of affairs in connection with the route."[3]

The Admiralty progressively disengaged from Larne after the war, and given the earlier correspondence with the Board about payment of rent and compensation, the Directors were no doubt relieved to note that the Royal Navy had paid dues of £7401-17-3, up to the end of September 1918. The Company bought a Naval Magazine for £25 at an Auction of Admiralty property, and the Chairman personally bought a Naval flag-pole with the intention of giving the Company an option "of securing it, if desired". The offer was politely refused on the grounds that "having no permanent site available, it might prove an obstruction."[4]

The Army was also disengaging from Larne, and the Company had a visit from a British Officer in the Spring of 1919 to discuss the rent owed for the military occupation of a field at Fleet Street, now a car park. The Officer was based in Dublin. Though the major changes in Ireland, due to Partition, were to have a profound effect on the historical development of the island, it is details like these which bring home the reality of the changes which such massive developments made to daily life on the ground.

Within a short time, all the Board's business with Government establishments would be dealt with in London or with the newly-established Northern Ireland Government based in Belfast. However in 1919 the Board still had to do business with the British Army establishment in Dublin, and agreed to take over the old military huts beside Fleet Street in Larne, plus a small hut at the wireless station, in lieu of £45 owed by the Army for rent. A year later, the Board was asked to subscribe to a fund for a Larne War Memorial, but declined to do so on the grounds that "all the Directors had already subscribed".[5]

On a human note, the Company's office-boy, who had had such a good war, continued to prosper. The Board noted on 20 October 1919 that as he "would complete his five years' service at the end of this month, it was agreed to increase his salary by £12 per annum, as from that date." Curiously, in all those years of Board Minutes he was never mentioned by name, which may be a reflection on the customs of the time when young people were not only unseen and unheard, but apparently also unnamed.

Miss Doag, another loyal servant, prospered steadily and on 26 February 1919, the Board agreed to raise her salary to £84 per annum. However, it is recorded in the Minutes of 28 April 1920 that a Miss McWilliam had been appointed to succeed Miss Doag "at a salary to commence at £50 per annum." It was reported that Miss Doag was leaving to get married, "after which she goes to Canada." The Board agreed to give her £5 as a wedding present.

Happily, however, the "boy" still prospered and in April 1920 the Board increased his salary by another £24 per annum "as more important duties would fall to him." Unhappily for the

Board, however, Miss McWilliam lacked the staying-power of Miss Doag, and she left the Company in the Spring of 1921.

The Board, ever anxious to help create new employment at Larne, agreed in the autumn of 1919 to meet a deputation from a trawling company wishing "to ascertain what facilities can be offered for the development of the fish business of this port." The Board indicated that it "was quite prepared to do anything reasonable in order to encourage trade to the port, and in the meantime the Board was prepared to grant a site for an ice factory in the field adjoining the Harbour Master's House." It also granted "liberty to erect an overhead system for the conveyance of ice from the factory to the ships, and a pipe connection underground with the sea, for the conveyance of sea water to the factory." The Board also agreed that if the fish business became well-established it would "consider any reasonable proposals for extra accommodation if required."[6]

The Board undertook to grant "a parcel of ground in the field adjacent to the Olderfleet Hotel . . . for a sum of £100 per annum" if the new company would agree to spend £5,000 on a new factory and plant. The Irish Trawlers Company Ltd, which was keen to set up the business, agreed to provide a guarantee of £1,000 per annum to help generate revenue for new berthing accommodation. A draft agreement between Larne Harbour Ltd and the Irish Trawlers Company Ltd was drawn up in May 1920, and at a special meeting on 19 July the same year, Larne Harbour accepted the agreement with Irish Trawlers, and this also required an agreement to the extension of a section of the quays.

However, there was an ominous lack of any mention in the Minutes of further progress on this venture, until the Board Meeting of 23 March 1921 when it was noted that "the work at the Ice Factory had been suspended." The Board had met representatives of the British Re-Inforced Concrete and Engineering Company Ltd, which was supplying steel and other material for the extension of the quays, "to consider the present position." The Chairman promised to discuss with the Company any possibility of them taking back "any of the re-inforcement not required."

The Larne Harbour Board were caught in a cleft stick, at a time when business was already bad. On 29 June 1921 the Board decided that "owing to the bad state of trade" the usual Twelfth of July gratuity for the staff would not be paid. At the same meeting the wages of the 'weekly men' were reduced by 2½d per hour, and in August it was decided that the wages of "piece and time workers" would be reduced by 12½ per cent from September, plus a further 6¼ per cent from 1 January 1922.

To make matters worse, the Anglo-American Oil Company Ltd decided in the Spring of 1922 not to proceed with the construction of an oil depot in Larne. The Company asked to be released from payment of rent but wanted to pay less than the total of £563-2-0 stipulated in their 12 year contract. The Board later offered to reduce the rent to £500. This situation dragged on, and the Anglo-Amercan Oil Co was finally released from its rental obligations in December 1926 on payment of £353-15-0. Clearly the Larne Board was no pushover.

However the dispute with the British Re-Inforced Concrete and Engineering Co was still to be settled, and the Larne Board decided on 22 May 1922 that any work on quay extensions should be postponed for another year "in consequence of the unsatisfactory state of affairs at present, and in view of still further reduction in wages and the cost of material."

Meanwhile, the British Re-Inforced Concrete and Engineering Co decided that it could not take back any of the material it had supplied to extend the quays, despite the failure of the Ice Factory. The row rumbled on, and in the Spring of 1923 the Larne Board met the Company to ask how the large sum of £7210-3-4 "for steel supplied in connection with the South End extension had been arrived at."[7] The parties failed to agree, and a Mr Chamberlain from Belfast Harbour was asked by the Larne Board to undertake an independent study. His fee was £25, plus 10 per cent "of anything recovered."

Some six months later Chamberlain reported back and concluded that the Larne Board had been overcharged by £4,000. The British Re-Inforced Concrete and Engineering Co declined to pay up, but offered to "do the next job for nothing." Chamberlain advised the Board to turn down this offer and to insist on a cash refund. Not surprisingly, the matter ended in the courts but it took a long time. Eventually, on 29 June 1927 the Board Minutes recorded that the Larne Harbour Company had been awarded £2,000 damages, plus £362-3-5 costs.

Mr Chamberlain was duly paid £200, as his agreed commission, and the Larne Harbour Ltd secretary was instructed forthwith to salt away £2,000 in War Stock – perhaps this was the larger part of the compensation sum! All this time the Board was also in dispute with the liquidator about the buildings left on the site of the proposed Ice Factory, and these were eventually sold to a Mr Allan McNeill early in 1928 for £325. All in all, it was a sorry end to a story which began with such hope and vision nearly nine years earlier.

Meanwhile, on the shipping front, the General Strike of 1926 brought further bad news to a depressed trade, and the Larne-Stranraer service was reduced, for a period, to three days a week – on Tuesdays, Thursdays and Saturdays. In the early and middle Twenties, the sea traffic remained in the doldrums, but towards the end of the decade, business began to pick up. This was partly because holidaymakers from the North of England and Scotland were becoming more ambitious, and more adventurous, in crossing the sea to Ireland.

There was also the paradox that despite the "Depression", coastal shipping was booming. This paradox was explained in some detail by Fraser G MacHaffie: "Unemployment was high – three million at one time – and between 1920 and 1922 average wages fell by an astounding 28 per cent, but prices fell by the same percentage in the same period. The decrease in wages continued until the graph reached its minimum point in June 1933, by which time the percentage drop on 1922 earnings was 12 per cent. But the significant feature of the Depression was that retail prices dropped by 24 per cent on the 1922 level, ie double the drop in wages. This meant that those in employment during the 1920s and early 1930s were better off in real terms and were enjoying a new affluence which enabled more ambitious holiday plans to be considered. The deflation also caused reduced fuel prices, lower building and crew costs, thus allowing fares to remain unchanged."[8] (It is no surprise

BELOW: Larne in the 1920's was the centre of a brisk trade in tourism. This letter, dated 9 June, 1926, offers to reserve 80 rooms at the Laharna Hotel, and 10 at the Old Midland Station Hotel for a conference being organised by a Mr John Earls, Principal of 'The Municipal College of Technology,' Belfast.

BOTTOM: The charges, outlined in an earlier letter of 26 April 1926 were obviously competitive – for example a double room at the Laharna would have cost 9/-, with another 9/- for breakfast, luncheon and 'meat tea'.

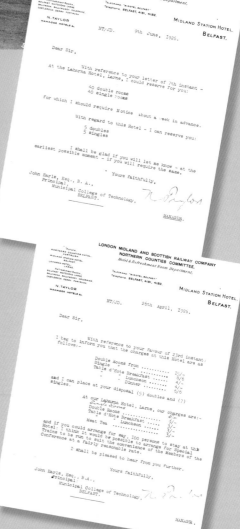

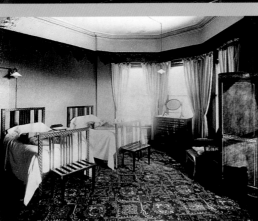

Portraits of the Olderfleet Hotel, circa 1936, by Alexander Hogg. These include a study of the lounge and a bedroom.

Pictures courtesy of The Ulster Museum. Top H01/67/13, Middle H01/67/15, Bottom H01/67/17

A W.A. Green study – the Princess Victoria leaving Larne for Stranraer in the 1920s. The tramp steamer Phyllis Seed is on the left.

Courtesy of the Ulster Folk and Transport Museum WAG 2564

that Mr MacHaffie later became a Professor of Accounting and Management at a College in Marietta, Ohio!)

To meet this increased demand, a new vessel was introduced on the Larne-Stranraer route. The Princess Margaret, built at a cost of £180,000, took over the mail run on 1 April, 1931. As in the past, each new vessel was an improvement on her predecessors, and the Princess Margaret was no exception. In contrast to the previous ships, "Princess Margaret could provide sleeping accommodation for 161 passengers – 107 in saloon cabins and 54 in steerage cabins. Of the saloon passengers, 53 could be accommodated in single cabins, while the remainder were in two-berth cabins. All cabins had hot and cold water. Deck machinery was electrically driven so as to minimise noise when cargo and mail was being loaded in the early morning.

"The rest of the ship was built to the best standards of the day. On the boat deck forward there was an observation lounge which extended the full width of the ship, while on this deck aft was a smoke room. Beneath the observation lounge was another lounge into which opened the offices of the purser and the night stewards. Also on this, the promenade deck, was a small pantry to provide early morning refreshments, while further aft was a dining saloon with seating for 54. On Princess Victoria and Princess Maud this deck had been almost completely open to the elements, apart from the shelter provided by the spar deck above. As was the custom with the earlier ships, the steerage accommodation was concentrated at the stern of the ship and was joined to the first-class accommodation by a gangway over the starboard side of the after hatch. On the poop deck were the baggage and mail rooms, as well as a smoke room and separate ladies' lounge. A general saloon with pantry and bar was situated on the main deck, while on the lower deck there was a dormitory with two-tier bunk beds.

"Below the main deck approximately 40,000 cubic feet of cargo could be stowed. Cattle stalls could be rigged to accommodate 236 beasts and, in addition, there were eight permanent horse stalls."[9]

In turn, the Princess Victoria was further overhauled at a cost of nearly £4,000 to try to aspire to the standards of her sister ship, but as part of the ill-luck which seemed to dog all the vessels of that name, she struck the Stranraer pier on her first day of service, and damaged herself. The old Princess Maud, which had been laid up at Stranraer was called out of semi-retirement to take over the Victoria's return sailing, but in dense fog she grounded at Barr's Point near the entrance to Larne Lough. Most of the 186 passengers and mail were landed by ship's boats, and the Maud was later sold off for £2,150 – quite an ignominious end for the old lady. Her master was severely censured for the mishap and not allowed to take command for the next twelve months.[10]

However, it was not long afterwards that another new vessel was commissioned for the route, at a cost of £160,000, and named, with a singular lack of imagination, the Princess Maud. She took over the mail service on 20 March, 1934. Soon after leaving Stranraer she passed the old Princess Victoria which was being towed to Norway for breaking-up. She had been sold for £3,000 and her last run was to Larne with a party of football supporters who had been to an international match in Glasgow.

The state of labour relations at the Harbour was a constant feature of Board meetings. The Company was a tough negotiator on wages and conditions, and yet tried to be considerate in certain circumstances. It negotiated an agreement with the Unions to provide a week's annual leave, and for many years it encouraged and contributed financially to an annual excursion (which continued until the late Sixties) for the men on a Saturday in June. It could also be helpful in individual cases.

Inaugural sailing of the Princess Margaret, 31 March 1931.

In September 1923 Captain Blair, the Harbour Master, had to resign "owing to failing sight", and the Board gave him a payment of £200 on leaving its service. In January 1932, William Beggs, a weighman, had to retire owing to ill-health after 42 years' service and asked the Company's "consideration for a small pension." He was granted 7/6 (seven shillings and sixpence) a week by the Board, the payment "to be made during the Directors' pleasure, and reserving the right to terminate the allowance at any time." Six months later the Board granted a pension of 10/- a week for one employee who

This view of Larne in the Twenties shows various vessels including – beyond the trees to the right – the prison ship Argenta.

had 50 years' service, and 7/6 a week for four others who had served for 45 years each. In August, 1932 a John Watson, aged 82, who had served for 54 years, was given a pension of 7/6 per week.

Collectively, however, the Board could strike a hard bargain. In May 1937, it expressed dissatisfaction with the coal fillers, and was considering dispensing with the jobs of eight men. The Board claimed that it was difficult to get the fillers to work overtime, and that part of the cargo of one ship had to be unloaded in Belfast because the Larne men refused to discharge it. In November 1937 a Union official asked the Board for an increase for fillers, crane-men and labourers. The Union subsequently reduced its claim, and asked for a rise for fillers only. The request for an extra half penny per ton was refused by the Board.

In March 1938, four workmen who had not paid their Union dues and were therefore out of benefit were dismissed by the Harbour Master Captain Close, "as the Harbour had agreed to employ only Trade Union men as permanent workers." A number of other men walked out in sympathy. Sir William Brown, a Director, told the Board that he had instructed the office staff to "make up (the men's) wages and send them by registered post, along with their Insurance Cards." The Board minutes of 22 March record that "Approval was given to the action taken."

The Company turned down the Union's predictable request for the men's reinstatement, but later the Board relented somewhat, and agreed to take back four of the fillers who "had probably been forced to leave their work." They were to be taken back as labourers "when it could be done." Later that month when the Union again requested the re-instatement it was told "As some of the men employed to fill the strikers' positions were not giving satisfaction, these men would be paid off, and some of our own men taken back."

It was agreed with the Unions that the position would be reviewed monthly. Nevertheless, in April 1939, a year after the incident had taken place, the Unions reminded the Board that some of the men who had gone on strike had not yet been re-instated. The Chairman informed the Unions that "on account of bad trade, we could not give full work to these men, but that at the times when we had required casual workers, any that had attended for employment had been given preference."

It was not only the workers who felt the rigours of sudden dismissal. Less than a week before Christmas 1934, the Secretary-Manager Mr Hugh Close was dismissed. Mr Alexander Larmour was appointed Secretary 'pro-tem' and he was instructed "to write to the Bank (sic) that the Company had dispensed with Mr Close's services from this date." It must have been a hammer-blow for one family in the run-up to Christmas, during a period of general depression and unemployment when a steady job was like gold dust.

Later that decade – on 16 August 1939 – another curt Minute records the dismissal of another senior employee, the Harbour Master, who earlier had dismissed the four men who had not paid their Union dues.

The Carrigan Head at Larne in the 1930's loading alumina for transportation to Canada, via the St. Lawrence.

The Board decided subsequently to give Captain Close three months salary in lieu of notice, though they pointed out that he was only legally entitled to one month. However, the Board insisted that he give up the Harbour Master's house within five weeks. The Company solicitor was told to "prepare a letter of termination and notice to quit his house."

It was also decided at this meeting to appoint Mr David Logan "to this position at a salary of £450 per annum, and free occupation of the Harbour House, also free electric light to the extent of £8 per annum." Mr Logan was to commence his duties on 1 October 1939 "or sooner if possible." His appointment was to prove to be much more than a significant footnote in the history of the Company.

All of this was played out against a background of great economic hardship in general. The historian Jonathan Bardon records some of the grim statistics:

A Tourist brochure with a print of a J. Humbert Craig picture of Larne Lough and the Chaine Tower.

"The Depression was unrelenting – this was no temporary downswing in the economy. Between 1931 and 1939, 27 per cent of the insured workforce was unemployed. The lowest point was reached in July 1935 when 101,967 in the region were out of work, but Northern Ireland's relative position was at its worst in 1938: in February of that year 29.5 per cent of insured industrial workers were unemployed as compared with 23.8 per cent in Wales, the highest figure for any region in Britain."[11]

Bardon's graphic account of the hardship of those times, including the hunger-marches and the severe counter-measures taken by the police, the poor housing conditions, and the desperation of the people to survive at a time of great hunger, illness and poverty, makes grim reading. At this remove, only some six decades later, and in an age of Northern Ireland affluence (by world standards), it is hard for younger generations to truly appreciate what their parents and grandparents had to endure.

The very fact that the Larne Harbour Company remained in business was an achievement in itself, given such a background. And yet, despite the poverty and the unemployment, there was an upsurge in demand for coastal shipping.

"In 1938 again new records were established. The overcrowding had become so blatant on the Irish routes that questions were asked in the House of Commons. The initial question cited the Glasgow-Londonderry sailings over the Glasgow Fair period, but soon the Glasgow and Ardrossan-Belfast and the Ardrossan-Isle of Man routes were also quoted as causing concern. Certainly this was an exceptional year on all routes to Belfast. Seven sailings were required to carry all the passengers seeking passage between Ardrossan and Belfast on the Saturday of the Glasgow Fair. At Heysham, 1,000 people were stranded at midnight of the last Friday in July (August Bank Holiday week-end) and had to be accommodated overnight in a Morecambe ballroom. The Stranraer route was under pressure.[12]

"The pressure being experienced at Stranraer at the peaks was cargo and motor cars. (In contrast to the other routes there was no cargo-only ship running parallel to the main passenger ships.) The shortness of the passage between Stranraer and Larne was being nullified by the time required to load and unload these items. The schedules for the peak days required each ship to give two double runs but, as we have observed, this was rarely accomplished as printed in the time-table.

"Car traffic continued to increase and jeopardise further the timekeeping of the steamers. In 1927, 600 cars were carried during July and August, in 1933, 2,000 cars were transported between June and September, while in 1937 over 4,000 cars made the crossing, the bulk of these being in the summer months. Nearly 5,500 were carried in 1938."[13]

Records for passengers and vehicles were being established and further established on the Larne-Stranraer route, as elsewhere across the Irish Sea, and it was no surprise when a new vessel was ordered. What was most significant, however, was the fact that "the LM and SR Board grasped the nettle and approved the building of their first cross-channel roll-on roll-off ferry. The Board approved expenditure of nearly £200,000 to provide terminals at Stranraer and Larne for a stern-loading vehicle and passenger ferry."[14]

The new vessel was named the Princess Victoria, and Fraser MacHaffie had the details:

"Princess Victoria was designed for carrying main passenger traffic as well as vehicles. The accommodation for the 1,400 passengers was situated entirely on the promenade deck with the exception of the ship's six staterooms (the only sleeping accommodation for passengers) on the boat deck. Buoyant seating was provided on the boat deck. Forward on the promenade deck first class passengers had a bar lounge and a dining saloon; while aft for third class passengers the same facilities were provided. The two identical dining saloons each had seating for 48 and shared a common pantry. Below the car deck was crew accommodation and stores space, and forward of the engines sheep pens were available. A simple docking bridge was built aft raised above the promenade deck and communicating with the main bridge by docking and starting telegraphs.

This postcard showing jaunting cars and a well-loaded two-horse carriage was sold by Lawrence publishing, Dublin.

"Another departure for the LM & SR was the engine-room; the Board had selected Princess Victoria to be their first diesel-propelled cross-channel vessel. One of her diesel engines was built by Sulzer Brothers, of Switzerland, and the other by Denny's under licence, and these combined to drive Princess Victoria at 19.93 knots when trials were conducted on 26 and 27 June 1939. The mean over six hours was 19.25 knots.

"Extensive alterations were made at both Stranraer and Larne to receive the revolutionary ship. At the Irish terminal, Spencer (Melksham) Limited had difficulties to surmount in their work of installing the electrically operated moveable ramp. The main difficulty was incorporating not one but two sets of railway lines that crossed at right angles to the ramp, and these two sets each had three lines because of the two gauges then applying in Ireland. The main ramp was 70 feet long and 10 feet wide and it was counterbalanced by weights. At the seaward end, the ramp had an 11 feet long hinged flap which could be adjusted independently of the main ramp. A 4 feet section connected the hinged flap to the stern of the ship. In addition to the ramp, a parking area was provided for 38 cars and a ticket office built. A conveyer for mail and luggage was installed between the ship's berth and Larne Harbour Station."[15]

The Princess Victoria took over the daylight service between Larne and Stranraer on 7 July 1939 and thereby inaugurated the prototype roll-on roll-off service which was to lead to the most significant development of the Port of Larne later on. Sadly, the development of this service was curtailed by the Second World War, which was declared on 3 September 1939.

Meanwhile, the Board of Larne Harbour Ltd carried on with its business as the war-clouds gathered. It was noted in the Minutes of 20 July 1938 that a suggestion had been received from the Northern Ireland Ministry of Commerce concerning harbour lighting and "that in the event of hostile action appearing to be imminent, the following lights should be exhibited only when required for berthing ships or for the guidance of vessels – namely the Railway Wharf leading lights."

At the Board Meeting of 15 February 1939 there was an item titled "Air Raid Shelters". The Secretary reported that "he had been asked by the Collector of Customs and Excise what protection had been provided for their men in the event of war, and that he had said that the protection of workers at the Harbour was under consideration." Some five months later, the Board noted in the Minutes of the meeting on 22 May that preparations had been made with the railway company for two connecting air raid shelters to be constructed at the back of the Harbour Office.

It is interesting to note that these indications of the impending conflict were reported in such a low-key manner. For example, the above item was followed by a Board Minute regarding an agreement with the Ministry of Finance to rent egg sheds at the Harbour "for three years at £18 per annum, and after that for £12 per annum." Clearly whatever the state of Europe, and it was in pretty poor shape by that stage, the business of the Harbour had to go on.

The Directors welcomed, with certain reservations, the bold new steps being taken by the railway company to build a modern ramp for the new ferry, Princess Victoria. At the Board

Meeting of 20 June 1939 the Directors noted anxiously "if the car ramp permanently ceased working, that a suggestion be made to the LMS to agree to take the ramp away and restore that portion of the quay to the state it was in before the ramp was built."

However, final approval was given on 18 July to the terms of the lease for the car ramp, especially as the Board had decided over a month earlier to consider the extension of the South End quay by some 40 feet "as the trade at the Harbour is steadily increasing and we may soon have frequent congestion." Some months earlier the Board had agreed to lease some land at the Harbour for a car park and ticket office, as well as space for refreshment rooms – all of which suggests that conditions must have been fairly primitive before then. The Board had also given permission for a Wesley Simpson to rent a stand for his two taxis at the Harbour at five shillings each, per annum. However this concession could be withdrawn at a week's notice, and the taxis were to remain in the vicinity of the ships for only a half-hour before or after the departure of the steamers.

To all intents and purposes the Harbour was quietly going about its business, gearing up its facilities and services to meet the increasing demands of a greater volume of passengers, and behaving, as far as possible, like a busy port in inevitably dwindling peacetime. The Second World War was to change all that, and after further years of bitter conflict for the second time in a bloody century, the face of Europe would not be the same again. Larne Harbour and its people would yet again endure conflict and undergo change, but the future was to be brighter than anyone dared to hope as the world plunged yet again into the darkness and horror of war.

1.   Op.Cit. Fraser G MacHaffie, pp110-112.
2.   Ibid, p112-113.
3.   Larne Harbour Ltd Minutes PRONI D3947/A/2.
4.   Op.Cit. 26 March 1919.
5.   Op.Cit. 16 February 1920.
6.   Op.Cit. 26 November 1919.
7.   Op.Cit. 11 May 1923.
8.   Op.Cit. Fraser G MacHaffie, p116.
9.   Ibid, pp117-118.
10.   Ibid, pp118-119.
11.   "A History of Ulster", p529, published by the Blackstaff Press Ltd, 1992.
12.   Op.Cit. Fraser G MacHaffie, p124.
13.   Ibid, p127.
14.   Ibid, p128.
15.   Ibid, pp128-129.

A morale-boosting visit to Larne during the Second World War by King George VI and Queen Elizabeth, now the Queen Mother. In this picture His Majesty greets Mr John Girvan, Mayor of Larne.

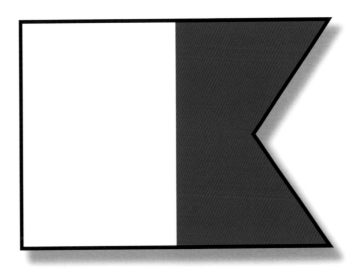

CHAPTER 6

IN THE EYE OF THE STORM

During the Second World War, the Port of Larne played a leading role as a major transit centre for troops and military supplies, and it thus made a significant contribution to the Allies' war effort. A much greater volume of traffic was handled than during the First World War, when the route between Kingstown and Holyhead was available. However this could no longer be used, due to the neutrality policy of the Irish Government, and a greater burden was placed on Larne and the other northern ports.

The story of the Port during this period of world upheaval is a striking combination of the harsh reality of war, and yet also the humdrum details of the management and administration of the Port. As thousands of American, British and other troops passed through Larne for service or special training in Northern Ireland prior to D-Day, and later set off for the savagery of the European battlefields, the Larne Harbour Board minutes contain details of such ordinary business as the long-running negotiations about harbour dues, the purchase of new equipment including everything from electric fires to a new tractor (which took several years to deliver due to war shortages), and also important milestones in the company's history – including the deaths of its long-serving chairman Charles MacKean and of his son Major WM MacKean MC, also a director, who was killed on active service in Italy. And although the daily business of the harbour often appeared mundane, there was always the underlying reality of hardship and danger, and of a world at war.

The Larne-Stranraer steamers Princess Victoria and Princess Maud were requisitioned almost immediately by the Admiralty, and within days of war being declared they set off for England. The Princess Victoria was never to return. On 21 May 1940 she struck a German mine in the Humber and sank, with the loss of 34 crew. The misfortunes which had dogged all the vessels named 'Princess Victoria' had struck again, with a vengeance.

The Princess Maud operated as a troop carrier between Southampton and France, and later was transferred to Dover. She took part in the Dunkirk evacuation, and on her first approach to the French port, an enemy shell tore a hole in her side and killed four of her crew. She limped back to England and after temporary repairs set off for France four days later and brought back 1,200 troops from Dunkirk. She also played a heroic role in evacuating men of the 51st Division from St Valery-en-Caux under heavy shelling. Once the evacuation of France was complete, the Princess Maud returned to Stranraer in the summer of 1940, and until November 1943 she transported troops between Scotland and Northern Ireland. In 1941 she was attacked and machine-gunned by an enemy aircraft returning from a bombing raid on Campbeltown, and one soldier was slightly wounded. The vessel received only superficial damage.

Near the end of 1943, the Princess Maud underwent alterations in Liverpool in preparation for the D-Day landings. On the night of 5 June 1944, she was part of the enormous convoy which left for the Normandy beaches, and in more than one trip she brought over 16,000 invading troops. Meanwhile, the Princess Margaret had been withdrawn from the mail run and converted into a commando ship. She sailed on D-Day with a destroyer escort and her role was to help in the destruction of heavy coastal batteries. She made several trips to the beaches and brought over the medical and nursing staff of one of the first medical units to be established in Normandy. She arrived back at Stranraer at the end of 1944 and once again took over the mail run, until the arrival of her sister ship the Princess Maud in September 1945. Clearly the Larne-Stranraer steamers had had a distinguished war.[1]

A number of other transport vessels came to Larne during the war and included the Canterbury, Maid of Orleans, Biarittz, Hampton Ferry, Shepperton Ferry, Twickenham Ferry, Royal Daffodil and Duchess of Hamilton. These were engaged solely in the transport of troops. When the Princess Margaret was taken to the south coast in 1944, the Royal Daffodil was used as a replacement on the mail service. The Royal Daffodil had been with the Princess Maud at Dunkirk, and also gave distinguished service as a Stranraer troop ship.

The three train ferries – the Hampton Ferry, the Shepperton Ferry and the Twickenham Ferry – could operate from the ramp already erected for loading the Princess Victoria. After the fall of France, the usefulness of these ships as train ferries had almost ceased, and they were about to be altered for other uses. The garrison in Northern Ireland was then steadily being increased, but great difficulty was being experienced in bringing ashore heavy equipment such as guns and tanks.

An official from the War office, with an astuteness not always found in Government offices, had the idea that if these ferries could be used between Larne and Stranraer, the problem would be solved. At short notice they were sent to Larne and were able to load and unload heavy military vehicles via the ramp. From July 1940, until their withdrawal before D-Day, they conveyed 92,000 vehicles as well as troops, and the main difficulty in equipping the garrison in Northern Ireland was removed. Churchill tanks manufactured in Belfast by Harland and Wolff Ltd were despatched in the same way, after reaching Larne in specially-constructed railway wagons. Trailers carrying hydrogen cylinders for the replenishment of the barrage balloon defences at Belfast and Londonderry were also conveyed by these ferries.

During much of the autumn of 1939, the military traffic passing through Larne consisted mainly of the despatch of territorial units to Great Britain. For a period only the mail steamer sailed by day, and the troops were transported after nightfall. Later as anti-submarine devices were improved, the policy was reversed and most of the shipping was done in daylight.

The first large troop movement through Larne was the intake of the 158th Infantry Brigade, numbering 2,700 men. Ships and the Port were for a time taxed to the utmost, as delays in the rail service to Stranraer resulted in many sailings falling behind time. The quantity of baggage far exceeded expectations, and included articles varying from a piano to a rowing boat. The war was then 'a Phoney War', and this, coupled with inexperience in handling the large volume of traffic, resulted in many unforeseen difficulties.

Better arrangements were made for the transport of the 53rd Division from South Wales in April 1940, but the efficiency that could only be acquired by experience was still lacking. This movement involved 374 officers, and 11,132 other ranks, with about 625 tons of equipment. The operation was extended over a period of 4 weeks, and required at least three troop trains and one baggage train each day at Larne Harbour. The utmost secrecy was maintained, but

During the Second World War Larne played a vital role as a major transit centre for troops and military supplies. These pictures show military vehicles being discharged around 1940 from one of the train ferries. It had been discovered that they could operate from the ramp erected just before the Second World War for the mail boat Princess Victoria. This was the first Roll-On/Roll-Off ramp at Larne Harbour. From July 1940 until their withdrawal before D-Day, the ferries conveyed 92,000 vehicles as well as troops. Between September 1939 until the end of the war more than 5 million service personnel and civilians passed through the port. The ramp was later demolished as part of the MacKean Quay Development.

Pictures courtesy of the Imperial War Museum, London

the file of correspondence at the Railway Superintendent's Office eventually reached a thickness of more than 2 inches. The units themselves were often unaware of their destinations, and had tickets made out in such terms as '9 W4', which caused at least one officer to refuse to surrender his ticket, as he had no means of satisfying himself that he had reached '9 W4'! More unfortunate was the officer, who held the view common to many Englishmen that Ireland was a practically uncivilised country, and who brought his men ashore with loaded rifles and fixed bayonets, expecting an attack from some wild Irish element on the Larne quayside.[2]

Meanwhile, the Board Minutes of Larne Harbour Ltd were very much in the mode of keeping the home fires burning. In November 1939 the Directors expressed their 'deep sense of loss' at the death of their 'colleague and friend' Sir William Brown. The Chairman wished to fill the vacancy reasonably quickly, but he was over-ruled, and not for the first time. It was not until the following May that Mr HJ Davison was co-opted as a Director.

Mr David Logan, referred to as 'Engineer and Manager' in a minute of 7 November 1939, was steadily prospering. He appeared to be a driving force in the Harbour, and had a hand in everything. For example, the minutes of 25 September 1940 record that permission was given to Mr Logan to buy three electric fires for the Harbour Office "as the military will not permit coal fires in the Harbour Office when petrol is being discharged at the North End." He was further empowered to purchase a typewriter at £40, and then as a juxtaposition to such relative minutiae, the records state that "Mr Logan was given permission to erect an air-raid shelter for his family."

The Board also showed a typical mixture of paternalism and hard-headedness. On 17 April 1940, the wages of Mrs McKinney, the charwoman, were raised from 7/6 per week to 10 shillings, while it was agreed to send half a ton of coal to a James Rea, "as this man appeared to be in poor circumstances." Later that year, in August, pensions were granted to Samuel Milligan, a waterman who received 7/6 a week, and the aforementioned James Rea, who also received a similar pension. At the same Board meeting, it was agreed to invest £2,000 in 2$\frac{1}{2}$ per cent National War Bonds. In January of that year, however, the Board – somewhat grudgingly – had paid £466-11-4 to the railway company for their share of the erection of three air-raid shelters, and noted rather huffily that "it was thought that the work could have been done for much less."

Early in 1941, David Logan was appointed Manager, following a probationary period of two months when he filled the vacancy caused by the dismissal of the previous incumbent. As was the custom, the details in the Board minutes were sketchy, but it appeared that he had deeply offended someone, possibly the company auditor Mr Rowan or the Chairman himself during a meeting with a military representative at the auditors' office concerning harbour business, and the penalty was instant dismissal.

Whatever the reason – and the Minutes give no real explanation – it was clear that David Logan was now firmly in charge, and his salary was increased to £500 per annum from 1 April 1941. Mr George Watson was appointed Secretary.

In May 1941 there were complaints about the "serious deterioration of the quays brought about by their constant use by large Government vessels", and in June the Board noted that work had begun on the construction of a North End War Department Extension. "Piles were being cast at Magheramorne, and material was arriving at the harbour." Around this time the military authorities tried to enlist the Board's help in paying for dredging, but they were less than enthusiastic at this stage. The Chairman spoke of "the decided decrease in imports and exports, and the limited means at the disposal of a small company."

The Harbour remained extremely busy, and some idea of the volume of traffic that passed through Larne may be seen from the following figures.

	Services Personnel	Civilians	Total
1 Sept – 31 Dec 1939	39, 997	21,229	61,226
1940	345,479	68,641	414,120
1941	738,048	134,904	872,952
1942	888,928	121,520	1,010,448
1943	811,543	100,378	911,921
1944	706,105	93,974	800,079
1945	777,822	213,557	991,379
TOTAL	4,307,922	754,203	5,062,125[3]

During all these operations there was never any serious accident. On only three occasions was the cross-channel service disrupted for reasons other than trains failing to run to time. Delay was caused twice by submarines in the channel, and in January 1945, Stranraer became snowbound, and as trains could not enter, the sailings were cancelled for a few days.

Unlike the conditions that prevailed during the first war, the ships made few deviations from the normal routes and sailed unescorted, and the anti-submarine campaign never assumed the proportions of 1914. The large fleet of trawlers was missing, as new methods in submarine detection reduced the number of ships required. A few ships equipped with radar and listening devices patrolled the narrow waters of the channel in the war against submarines, while improved aircraft technology, between the wars, enabled a more efficient air cover to be maintained.

The pre-war luxury yacht, Philante, was stationed at Larne as a submarine depot ship, accompanied by light coastal craft and an occasional drifter. After the War, the "Philante" was sold to the Norwegian Royal Family and named the KV "Norge" – to become their Royal Yacht. She was built for Sir Thomas Sopwith in 1937 and was (for a time) the largest motor yacht ever built in Britain. During the War she covered an immense mileage and her final duty and surely her most triumphant, was to escort surrendered German submarines into Loch Eriboll in Scotland. The trawler Stella Orion operated from Larne during the early days of the

This picture shows, centre and left, the remains of a Second World War air raid shelter. On the right is a fleeting glimpse of the P&O Jetliner in 1999 as she sets off on her one hour journey to Cairnryan.

war, and was later sunk on active service. The Olderfleet Hotel was again taken over by the Naval authorities becoming known as HMS Racer, as well as the Olderfleet Quay, and Larne became one of the principal training centres for crews engaged on anti-submarine warfare.

There was, however, no large floating population as there had been in the first war – large numbers of naval personnel being no longer required. After the fall of France a strange visitor came to Larne Lough in the Free French dredger, Victor Gilloux. The crew of this vessel had responded to the call made by General de Gaulle, and had sailed to a British port and placed themselves at the disposal of the Allies. Dredgers were, however, vessels that could not be used to the same extent in war as in peace, and there appears to have been some difficulty in deciding where to send the Victor Gilloux. Eventually she came to Larne and spent a period dredging the shallow parts of the lough. She was a ship of considerable size, and, fitted with powerful suction apparatus, she was a contrast to the more usual crane and bucket dredger. During the dredging operations, objects such as ancient anchors, cannon balls, and portions of old wooden ships were brought to light, evidence of the many and varied types of ships that formerly came to Larne.

Throughout the war years the rail and road services at Larne bore a continuous strain, due to the volume of traffic. The Harbour station, itself never commodious, and handicapped by the presence of the level crossing, had its space further restricted by the erection of offices for Movement Control, for Home Office emigration, and by the construction on the outer platform of an improvised kitchen and canteen for troops. The position was eased by using the cattle dock or old passenger platform, as a platform for troop trains, this being made possible by the cessation of cattle traffic. Trains carrying large numbers of Italian and German prisoners of war also used the cattle dock. Carriage storage accommodation was also increased by putting a third rail on the narrow gauge line, and this three-legged track proved invaluable. Mr Robert Mackerell, who was station master at Larne throughout the war period, was recognised for his work by the award of the British Empire Medal.

There was also a substantial canteen built on Fleet Street, behind the Olderfleet Hotel (HMS Racer) which provided tea, sandwiches, and entertainments for a considerable number of service personnel. It was organised by the WVS but many of the local womenfolk helped on a voluntary rota basis, including Mrs Jim McCarlie and Mrs David Logan. After the War, this hall housed a knitting industry, and later it was run by a local Committee to provide various entertainments, including dances and whist drives.

Early in the war it was obvious that the berthing accommodation was insufficient. The middle and north berths were almost continuously occupied by cargo vessels, and the mail berth was hard-pressed to cope with the mail boat and also the special military sailings.

Thousands of American troops passed through Larne during the Second World War. This is Milburn Henke, the first G.I. to step on Ulster soil in 1942.

Picture courtesy of Belfast Telegraph

To provide for the increasing traffic, the War Department decided to build a new pier in concrete to the north of the existing berths. The work required the removal of some old landmarks, including the eighteenth century slaughter house, and much of the residence and garden occupied for generations by the McNeill family. Embodied in the design of the pier was a hand-operated ramp to enable it to be used by the ferries. The new pier which came to be known as the 'Continental Quay', was ready for use in 1943, but owing to its exposed position it was never used by store ships and only by the ferries when the mail boat berth was not available. It was extensively used, however, for special military sailings as it avoided the undesirable former practice of double banking vessels. The new pier was provided with two railway lines, on which four-wheeled vehicles and certain classes of railway engines could work. On account of the heavy curvature, however,

ABOVE: Construction of the railway to Continental Quay during the Second World War, with a narrow gauge locomotive and broad gauge wagon. The building on the left previously housed the offices of Larne Harbour Ltd.

ABOVE: The completed Continental Quay in the early Forties.

Pictures courtesy of the Imperial War Museum, London

LEFT: The view from the north end of the Harbour about 1940, prior to the construction of the Continental Quay. The old slaughter-house is in the foreground, left, and in the far distance is the Chaine Tower. A Larne-Stranraer vessel is offshore.

carriages could not be taken to the pier. The new connecting line through the goods yard became known as the 'Burma Road', owing to the fact that it was built before the Japanese invasion of Malaya and Burma, when the road through Burma was the principal link with China.

Petrol for military purposes was imported in large quantities and sent from Larne to the army depots at Randalstown, Limavady and Scarva. Contrary to the general method employed in shipping petrol, this was brought in cans aboard coasting vessels, and taken away immediately from the quayside. Tankers could have been used and the petrol passed through the depot of Messrs Holmes, Mullin and Dunn, already established beside the Olderfleet Hotel. However, this method was not adopted, as tankers were in short supply and there were not enough petrol-carrying lorries and railway wagons to move the cargo quickly. Perhaps the most important reason for this arrangement was the possibility of air raids on the Port. It was not considered advisable to permit petrol to remain overnight at Larne. A large percentage of the petrol cans were leaky, and this caused much inconvenience in discharging from the ships and reloading to railway wagons. The cans were loaded by hand in the hold of the ship, a dangerous and difficult operation. Those that leaked were brought ashore separately and their contents pumped into road tankers. Between August 1940 and December 1945, 9,475 wagons containing 68,701 tons of petrol were discharged at the Randalstown depot, and most of this came through Larne.

The first American troops arrived in Belfast on 26 January 1942 to a warm welcome, which included the band of the Royal Ulster Rifles playing 'The Star-Spangled Banner'. By May of that year there were 37,000 American troops in Northern Ireland and, according to historian Jonathan Bardon, "for a time there were 120,000 Americans in the North."[4] In the autumn of 1943 they began to arrive in Larne in large numbers.

Trains from Larne Harbour during October 1943 carried American troops to Poyntzpass and Banbridge, and to Omagh and Tandragee. Times had changed, and the old song was outdated. Philadephia was coming back to Ireland in the morning, and the almost silent shuffle of American rubber-soled shoes presented a contrast to British nailed boots.

Dockers and railwaymen alike were smoking Camels and Lucky Strikes, distributed freely by the affluent Americans, many of whom appear to have thought they were coming to a country that was on the verge of starvation.

The Americans made a big impression on the locals, in all sorts of ways. Mrs Hester McGarel, the wife of Mr Archie McGarel who was later a member of the Larne Harbour management team, tells the story of her mother who was then working as a nurse-maid to a family living on Chaine Road. "My mother told us that one day there was a knock on the door, and an American soldier with a black cocker-spaniel said to her 'We are not allowed to take animals with us, could you find a home for this dog?' My mother said 'I suppose so', and she brought the dog home. Apparently it must have been involved in training when the troops were firing their guns because it was so nervous that it shuddered at any loud sound like a door jamming. It became a family pet, and everybody loved it!"

When the American troops were being moved from Northern Ireland in the spring of 1944, Larne was particularly useful, as ships could sail on any tide. Trains carrying troops to other ports had, in many cases, to be carefully arranged, as some of the larger ships could only sail on the high water, and to miss a tide might mean a delay of up to 12 hours.

The invasion of France and the liberation of the Low countries brought the Belgians to Larne, mostly young men of military age. They were enrolled in their own units of the Belgian army, and though British battledress was the usual uniform, it was the uniform of necessity, as these Belgians had little equipment and were dependent on the British Army authorities. Their coming to Larne was thus different from that of the British and American troops who had preceded them. They had little more than the clothes in which they stood, and many bore traces of the effects of the German occupation. When they left in their new uniforms, they were different men.

Charles MacKean, Chairman of Larne Harbour Ltd from its inaugural meeting in 1912 until his death in 1943. 'His charming disposition, amiable personality and sterling qualities endeared him to all.'

Picture courtesy of Mrs Patricia MacKean

Mrs McGarel recalls a concert for the Belgians in the Victoria Hall, at which her friend sang a solo while wearing the Belgian national colours. "It helped to make them feel at home."

While history was being made in Europe, the Larne Harbour Board had to contend with sombre events at home. On 18 December 1943 its long-serving Chairman Charles MacKean died, and the Directors paid a fulsome tribute to him at the next Board meeting, on 14 January 1944. They noted that "his charming disposition, amiable personality and sterling qualities endeared him to all." He had given exceptional service to the company and had remained in the Chair since the initial meeting in 1912. During the succeeding 31 years he rarely missed a meeting, and he played a major role in guiding the company through the momentous events of the times, both in war and peace. He was succeeded by HJ Davison, who was appointed at the Board meeting of 15 March, but sadly his tenure of office was extremely short, and following his sudden death, HT Browne's appointment as Chairman was confirmed by the Board on 19 April 1944. A week later, James McClenaghan was co-opted to the Board to fill the vacancy caused by the death of Mr Davison. At the same Board meeting, on 25 April 1944, Captain William Muir MacKean MC was co-opted to fill the vacancy left by his father Charles, and "for the period of the war he was granted leave of absence." Tragically, however, he was killed a few months later while on active service in Italy, and the Board, at its meeting of 18 October 1944, sadly passed on its condolences to his family.

As the War dragged on, the Larne Board and the Admiralty were still haggling over harbour dues, but the Board steadily increased its employees' wages, and even felt able to give a £5 gratuity to a retiring trade union official. In March 1945, the Board introduced compulsory retirement at the age of 70, and on 4 April compulsorily retired its foreman John Campbell on a pension "of thirty shillings per week." The Board minute stated also that "It was agreed to dispense with the services of two watchmen who had reached the age limit, namely Richard and John Armstrong."

By mid-summer of 1945, the increasing return to normality was underlined by a Board minute on air raid shelters – "of the 11 erected, it was agreed to retain three and to arrange for the demolition of the remainder." The Board noted that the net profit for the year ending 31 March 1945 was £6,945-10-11, excluding a 4 per cent tax-free dividend for the Directors. This was in stark contrast to the paper profit of the transport operators who used the port.

"It is not always appreciated what a windfall a war or similar crisis can be to transport operators. The profit for the Stranraer service in 1939 was £16,800 with gross receipts of £98,000. . . . In 1940 gross receipts of £139,000 . . . produced a profit of £72,000. Thereafter the operating profit, gross receipts and passengers carried continued upwards, apart from the setback in 1944, until in 1945 . . . the gross receipts of £326,000 produced a profit of £186,000. A considerable proportion of the greatly increased profit was made possible by the nature of the traffic, since the usual seasonal peak was flattened. For example, in 1938, 50 per cent of the passenger traffic used the route in the eight weeks to 7 August, whereas in 1940 only 25 per cent of the year's travellers crossed in the corresponding period.

"But the increased income from the mail steamer and the benefits of the levelling of seasonal peaks did not accrue directly to the LM & SR. The major railway undertakings of Britain came under Government control from 1 September 1939 and thereafter all revenue of the railways (from all activities except road haulage) was pooled and an annual payment made to the companies by the Government. The formula employed required that of the first £43 1/2 million of revenue, payment to the companies was based on the average net revenue for the three years 1935-37. The LM & SR received 34 per cent of this £43 1/2 million. Any surplus over the £43 1/2 million was split – half to the Exchequer and half to the railway companies."[5]

As the war drew to a close, and the number of troops and volume of transport decreased, the port began to revert to its pre-war activity. The Naval base was closed in 1945, and the Board minute of 27 June records a warm tribute from the Naval Officer-in-Charge, Captain Fothergill RN. He wrote "On the closing down of the Naval Base at Larne, I wish to express my appreciation of the ready assistance we have received from your manager, Mr Logan, and the staff of Larne Harbour Board. This happy co-operation has greatly helped us to play our part in the war, and we are indeed deeply grateful."

The Port of Larne, and its people, had once again risen to the challenge of war. It was now time to face the considerable challenges and opportunities of peacetime.

1.   Op.Cit. Fraser G MacHaffie, pp131-134.
2.   "The Second World War" – A short unpublished history of Larne Port, now in the possession of Larne Harbour Ltd.
3.   Ibid. Also see The Operating Department in War-Time 1939-45 (Belfast: London Midland and Scottish Railway Northern Counties Committee, 1946), p51.
4.   Op.Cit. Jonathan Bardon, pp574-575.
5.   Op.Cit. Fraser G MacHaffie, pp133-134.

The Islandmagee ferry crammed with VIPs, including Sir Basil Brooke, later Lord Brookeborough, the Prime Minister of Northern Ireland (middle right). In the background, standing with cap, is Sammy McCalmont, one of the ferrymen.

The opening of the first Ballylumford Power Station in 1945, with Sir Basil Brooke (right) – complete with cigarette in the days when it was politically correct to smoke in public.

Pictures courtesy of A & C Photography, Belfast

Colonel Frank Bustard, whose vision for a new system of moving goods in bulk led to the development of Larne as a major ferry and container port.

Picture courtesy of Arthur Winter, Preston

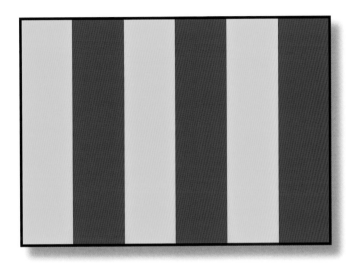

CHAPTER 7

NEW HORIZONS

Although Larne had been a thriving port during the Second World War, it experienced a short post-war decline in tonnage and shipping. The closure of the British Aluminium Company in 1947 was a blow to the town, and also to the Port. The Board of Larne Harbour Ltd and its general manager David Logan set out to attract new business, and when Lieutenant-Colonel Frank Bustard approached the company with the proposal for a new commercial service between Larne and Preston, his ideas were accepted with alacrity. This in turn led to a massive development of the commercial business which was to bring such prosperity to the Port. It could be argued, in fact, that the arrival of Colonel Bustard was as significant for Larne as that of James Chaine roughly three quarters of a century earlier.

The relative decline of Larne in the early post-war years is illustrated from the records of Larne Harbour Ltd. The number of vessels decreased from 1,517 in 1936 to 1,227 a decade later. In 1946 the net registered tonnage was 685,718 compared to 722,783 in 1936. In 1938 the net registered tonnage of foreign, coastwise and Larne-Stranraer vessels was 712,982 compared to 542,862 in 1947.

One observer stated: ". . . the most noticeable drop between the two years was in foreign shipping – in 1947 it was only 17 per cent of 1938's figures, while for coastwise shipping the figure was little more than 50 per cent. Imports of goods had fallen more noticeably than exports, this being attributable to the closing of the alumina factory in 1947".[1]

The anxiety about the loss of trade was mirrored in the Board Minutes of Larne Harbour Ltd, at a time when the company was grappling with the problems of storm damage at the mail steamer berth, a much-needed revision of harbour tonnage dues, and the negotiation of a final settlement of £15,000 from the Ministry of Transport for damage done to the berth by Government vehicles. On 10 December, the Board agreed a 44-hour week for Port workers, but on 14 January, 1948 it refused an application for increased wages "in view of the serious trading position of the company."[2]

As early as 31 July 1946, the Board was eager to attract new business. It had bought the Corran property nearby, which included over 10 acres of land, for £8,000 just over a month earlier, and asked the Northern Ireland Ministry of Commerce "to use their endeavours to interest some of the cross-channel firms who are on the look-out for suitable sites for industry." They did succeed in this eventually, and the Pye Radio factory was established, which provided training and employment for many workers in Larne, including some returning from war service. The factory was extremely modern, for its day, and some of the buildings are still in use, around 50 years later. The Pye factory was later to close, partly due to the development of hi-technology in the Far East, and ironically, much of the recent drive for inward investment to Northern Ireland has been targeted at hi-technology companies overseas. The factory was eventually used to accommodate another company, Standard Telephones and Cables.

Significantly, a Board Minute of 26 November, 1947 carried the first reference to a hopeful new chapter in the history of Larne Harbour. It referred to "An inspection of the WD Pier by Colonel Bustard, accompanied by Mr McCleery of LM and S Railway with the object of inaugurating a Motor Ferry Transport Service between Preston and Larne Harbour. It was reported that Col. Bustard was favourably impressed with the ramp, water and general conditions at Larne Harbour. After a full discussion it was agreed that Mr Logan should arrange an interview with Col. Bustard at Tilbury, taking the requisite plans with him and ascertain when there, what charges are being levied for handling."

David Logan visited Tilbury without delay. The Board noted on 17 December: "After discussions at Tilbury and London regarding a Preston-Larne service, it was decided that the WD Pier would be suitable and that Larne Harbour would make the necessary arrangements. Col Bustard was of the opinion that he would be a position to start the service early in the New Year." Clearly they were in business, though it took several months longer than Bustard had anticipated to get the new service going.

Frank Bustard was an impressive character, with the entrepreneurial flair of an early Richard Branson. He had planned to introduce an efficient cut-price ocean liner service on the North Atlantic before the Second World War, and the failure of this ambitious idea – through no fault of his own – led him after the War to consider other ambitious projects, to the good fortune of Larne.

He was born in Liverpool on 20 February, 1886. The story of his youth and of his attempts to establish the Atlantic Steam Navigation Company Ltd is well-chronicled by Miles Cowsill in his history of the company titled "By Road Across the Sea."

"On leaving school at the age of 16, he joined the then White Star Line as the last of the company's office apprentices. As a postage clerk he earned 5/- (25p) a week working 13 hours a day. Later, at the age of 21, he was appointed as the Chief Assistant to the Passenger Department Manager (Second and Third Class steerage).

"By 1934, Frank Bustard was the Passenger Traffic Manager. In the same year, the Government merged Cunard Line with White Star Line. He was asked by the Directors of both companies to accept service with the new merged operation, but he declined, as he felt that his old company would soon be entirely submerged and Cunard would become the prominent operating name. How right he was!

"Frank Bustard felt that Cunard would be entirely opposed to his ideas for broadening the approach to travel on the Northern Atlantic with cheaper fares. He felt now was the right time for cheaper fares, to offer more opportunities for people to travel on the Atlantic. He planned to offer a one-way fare of £10 on his new service, with a la carte menus as an extra, similar to some of the Atlantic air services developed in the Eighties."

He left Oceanic House and opened his own office in Norway House, opposite the old White Star Offices. He employed three ex-White Star Line employees, and two years later, the Atlantic Steam Navigation Company Limited was formed. A new North Atlantic shipping company was not welcomed by the Government of the day, since it would mean competition for the newly-formed Cunard White Star Line.

Following the formation of the Company, he set about negotiating the acquisition of vessels to operate his new service, but he was unsuccessful.

"In view of this outcome, he decided to have designs prepared for two liners for his Atlantic service, and he approached Vickers Armstrong. The two liners were designed to carry 1,500 passengers in two classes (Cabin and Tourist). Two very attractive three-funnelled ships of about 33,000 gross tons were designed, with a service speed of 22 knots.

"By late 1936 it was rumoured that the new vessels were to be named Silverswift and Silverfalcon. With a contract price of £2.25 million per vessel and tentative delivery dates agreed, ASN proposed sailings from Liverpool to New York via Dun Laoghaire every 10 days. The project was complete."

In October 1938, Bustard approached the Bank of England for financial assistance but, due to the negative attitude of the Government, his request for a loan of £2.5 million was turned down.

"Frank Bustard pursued his project nevertheless with undaunted determination, even approaching the established shipping companies Orient and Anchor Lines with his plans. Events in Europe were to overtake the new Company's plans, with the Munich crisis and finally the outbreak of the Second World War in 1939."[3]

Frank Bustard was called up for the Army Reserve, and when the war ended he was in his 60th year, at an age when other men might have thought of a gradual down-changing of gear towards retirement. However, age was no barrier to this entrepreneur and he turned his creative mind to further business. He tried to resurrect his ambitious and visionary plans for a cost-cutting North Atlantic service, but he soon realised that the world had changed, and no suitable ships were readily available.

Instead, he turned his attention to the possibilities offered by converted Naval tank landing ships (LST's) which had made such a significant contribution to the Allied invasion of Europe. The transport of tanks and other heavy equipment was not well-suited to conventional vessels, but the LST's were specially designed for the discharge of military vehicles over their bow ramps onto the sands of the Normandy beaches. It is estimated that from July 1944 to May 1945 inclusive, 43 per cent of the heavy military vehicles which crossed the channel were taken by LST's.[4]

Bustard, together with Don Smith of the Liverpool stevedoring firm of Smith Coggins Ltd, had witnessed the early beaching trials of these ungainly vessels on New Brighton Sands in 1943 and they both came to the conclusion that when the War ended, these could be adapted to carry cargo driven on board. Thus began, in simple form, the Roll-On/Roll-Off (RO/RO) revolution.

Frank Bustard who had so clearly seen the potential, set about briskly to turn his vision into reality. After long negotiations with the Ministry of War Transport, the Admiralty and the War Office, he was allowed to charter (at very favourable terms) three LST's – numbers 3519,

The SS Empire Cedric (top), Empire Gaelic (middle) and Empire Doric (bottom). All three were former Tank landing craft of the kind used in World War II, and later modified for commercial ferry traffic. Some of these were later requisitioned for service during the Suez Canal crisis in 1956.

3534 and 3512 which became respectively the Empire Baltic, Empire Cedric and Empire Celtic. According to one source it was a neat irony that the names perpetuated those of the old White Star line, which Frank Bustard had joined at the age of 16!

He was later to record his debt to the Labour Government, "without which he was convinced that the revolution in sea transport which he initiated would never have taken place, certainly at that time. Government provided the ships, but Bustard and his backers had to raise the money for fitting them out and providing crew accommodation on board."[5]

Not surprisingly, Bustard raised the money, and his new venture, which later became known as the Transport Ferry Service, gradually established itself – but not without hard work and some early hitches. The Colonel's son Michael Bustard, who was to play a key role in the new operation, recalls that the Government , playing fair with all sides, invited established British shipowners to witness a RO/RO demonstration at Tilbury, but they dismissed the idea and literally left the seas open to ASN.[6]

The new charters had to undergo modification, including improved accommodation, alterations in the engine room and boiler room, and modified funnels and navigational aids. One of the problems of those early days was the lack of any ASN working capital, but fortunately there was a workshop at Tilbury operated by Harland and Wolff Ltd of Belfast, which had had such a strong pre-war connection with the White Star Line. Michael Bustard later paid tribute to Harland and Wolff. "Without their unstinted financial assistance, especially for the conversion of the first three vessels . . . it is doubtful if ASN would have survived those early anxious days at Tilbury."[7]

The first sailing took place on 11 September 1946 when the Empire Baltic, under the command of Captain JW Rennie, crossed from Tilbury to Rotterdam with a cargo of new vehicles for the Dutch Government. Michael Bustard, who took part in that voyage, recalled some of the early hazards, and inconveniences.

"The voyage to Rotterdam in those days was good for 24 hours and we did not pass the Hook of Holland until early the following morning, finally arriving at our "berth", nothing more than a deserted sandy beach near the Waalhaven, at 10 am. There was no quay alongside, no shore hard, just nothing – the ship being held by the stern anchor. Before the ramp could be lowered, the two bow doors had to be opened and before they could be opened the beams holding them together had to be unbolted and removed. This process took at least an hour, with a new and untrained crew.

"Eventually, the bow doors slowly opened, only to find that the bottom corners of the port door stuck in the sandy bottom of the beach. The hero of the day – a Mr Bottomley of Messrs Smith, Coggins, our stevedores – called for a spade and jumping into the water fully clothed immediately began to shovel sand away some 4' below the surface of the water. Eventually the door freed itself, thanks, I suspect, more to the tipping of the ship than to his digging efforts; the bow ramp came down and the cargo of lorries was driven ashore – getting rather wet in the process. The whole operation took place in this rather desolate section of the Port of Rotterdam against a skyline of heavily blitzed warehouses, and I well remember the only spectators of this historic occasion were some rather thin and hungry looking Dutch boys leaning on the handle-bars of their bicycles.

"Although the operation of discharge was complete by lunch-time, there was no question of any speedy return to Tilbury and orders were given for the ship to sail again at 8 am the following morning. The first few voyages of the Company's ships followed this rather leisurely pattern of operation and any attempts to speed up the process were usually demolished by vague – but no less ominous – references to the need for an overnight examination of the boilers. . . .

"Other rigours suffered in the early days included the complete absence of any plumbing in the cabins. Passengers shared the Officers' bathroom, where three washbasins and the one bath were all in the same room – the bath being discreetly, but ineffectively, screened off by a green canvas curtain. For passengers, however the most fearsome trial of all was the dreaded "outside" cabins, to which access could only be gained by going outside on to the dark and open Upper Deck, dodging the rain as best one could. Once in there for the night, access to the more convenient parts of the ship was difficult, if not impossible, without the exasperation of getting fully dressed again."[8]

The service prospered, using the three chartered vessels, and these were joined in 1948 by a similar vessel, the Empire Doric. The ASN later switched the service to Hamburg and then, in 1955, to Antwerp. Meanwhile, Frank Bustard turned his attention to the Irish Sea route. Originally he had intended to operate this new service from Liverpool, but the idea was opposed by other operators using the port, and the company turned to Preston which, like Larne, welcomed them. Despite its operational difficulties as a tidal port, Preston was a focus for road hauliers at that time and its empty coal siding provided excellent parking space.

The Empire Cedric initiated the service with its inaugural sailing on 21 May 1948. Captain HT Green, who joined the Company in 1947, recalls the first voyage.

Captain William Close took up a post with the new Transport Ferry Service between Larne and Preston. He joined the Empire Cedric and later, the Empire Gaelic before becoming Master, in 1954, of the Empire Doric.

"Pioneering the Roll-On/Roll-Off service at Preston – the first of its kind in the world – gave one a great deal of satisfaction and many heartaches. We had to learn and learn fast. Apart from trouble with the pontoon at Preston which, being water ballasted and not sub-divided, tipped whichever way the water ran, our first arrival at Larne was somewhat of a fiasco. Crowds on the quay, the "red carpet" treatment – to find the shore linkspan would not connect but by dint of rapid work on the part of a burner, the offending parts were cut away and all was well. Our faces were a bit red at the time but it was our first introduction to Davey Logan who was a master of improvisation."[9]

John Jolly, right, a senior member of the Staff of Transport Ferry Service, based in Preston with David Logan, Manager of Larne Harbour.

Mr John Jolly, a member of the shore staff at Preston describes the development of the service "The first cargo carried comprised 14 items and two lorries each carrying 65 gas cookers which were shipped on this voyage on behalf of Messrs Moffats of Blackburn and must logically have been the first two commercial vehicles in the world to have been carried in this manner as freight.

"At this stage we were looked upon as "Adventurers" and not "Venturers" by the Port Authorities, and the shipping fraternity gave us only six months to live. Shortly after the commencement of the Irish Service we obtained a contract to carry some 2,000 pre-fabricated houses, loose, like a pack of cards, on trailers for erection in Larne. One of our original and most interesting cargoes in the early days was the carrying of Messrs Pilkington lorries loaded with sheet glass which again was the first time that glass has been carried in this manner by sea. This became a most valuable selling point to us, for in over twelve months we never cracked a single pane whereas by the conventional method of shipping their breakages had averaged 25% per annum. The first circus we carried was from Larne to Preston, a small Irish company named Sandow's Circus."[10]

Despite such varied and exotic cargoes, Michael Bustard remembers that the first few sailings were disappointing. "On some nights only one or two vehicles were carried. Traffic was agonisingly slow to build up. But still the ships sailed on at a loss. It took two years for the traffic to build up to justify a third ship on the service."[11]

In 1950 the service was extended to Belfast, and the Empire Gaelic joined the fleet. Within a short time the sailings from Preston were increased to six or seven a week to the two ports. The service, despite the early scepticism of seasoned operators, was proving itself. Captain William Close from Larne, who was one of the best-known captains on the service, provided a graphic (and somewhat poetic) account of its gradual success, despite the difficulties of navigating the River Ribble!

"The initial years up to 1956 were a time of great job satisfaction. One was aware of contributing to the success of a new venture and almost every week another customer would arrive. A great deal of the traffic was by companies using their own transport, and their vehicles were generally immaculate, in showroom condition. The drivers were company employees of long standing usually in a smart uniform and travelling weekly year after year.

"The voyage in the LSTs could in itself be quite an adventure. Normally the overall passage time was about 14 1/2 hours. The sea passage was about 12 hours at 10 1/2 knots, and 2 1/2 hours were spent negotiating the River and locks, arriving at or departing from Preston.

The Empire Gaelic discharging the first vehicle to come over the new 120 ton ramp at Curran Quay in 1956.

"In bad weather it could take much longer. The LSTs had a very quick rolling motion. To minimise this and protect the cargo it was the practice to keep heading into the sea until one could turn the ship as quickly as possible bringing the sea astern. This might add many hours to the passage. One frequently had to run for shelter and we must have anchored in most of the various bays in the Irish Sea.

"A winter voyage could last for days rather than hours. I think a week was the record for a round voyage. However, this was generally accepted philosophically by all concerned. There was considerable satisfaction in having, as it were, weathered the tempest and attained a safe anchorage, there to await it blowing itself out.

"Navigation of the Ribble commenced at the Gut buoy about 16½ miles from the dock entrance. The channel was enclosed by retaining walls for much of its length. It was marked by buoys at the entrance and lighted perches for the rest of its length. In the early days many of these were lit by paraffin lamps like those on a Victorian railway platform. After a strong blow many would be extinguished to be re-lit in a leisurely fashion by the "lampies" whose sole job it was to maintain them.

"One arrived at the Nelson buoy about two hours to high water and the River passage and locking in varied from 1½ hours to three hours depending on the state of the tide, other traffic etc, but normally lasted about two hours.

"Negotiating the stretch from Wallend buoy to Lytham in a West to North Westerly gale was an unforgettable experience.

"A very big breaking sea developed over the Bar and one had to be very alert and sure of one's judgement to clear the sandbanks to the North and avoid being carried over the Wall to the South by leeway and tide which, once the wall and banks were covered, ran strongly in an East-South Easterly direction. Keeping as close to Salters buoy as possible one made about a 30° alteration to port to avoid the South bank which was liable to encroach into the channel, and shortly after a similar turn to starboard. Often, after bad weather, one or more of the buoys would be missing and the seaward perch demolished, so that one was compelled to judge the position by keeping the bearings of perches open to clear the wall.

"It was an exercise which could not have been attempted without confidence in the ship, one's local knowledge and the ability of the quartermasters to steer accurately a given course. It was a great relief, but very satisfying, when one gained shelter approaching Lytham and could take in the stabilisers. After Lytham the River became canal-like and the main concern was outward traffic, sand pumps or often a combination of both.

"The upper reaches were surrounded by extensive marshes on both sides. On a calm summer's morning these would be covered by low-lying mist above which showed the tops of solitary trees giving an unreal impression of a world of primeval swamps at the dawn of time. At that time there was a great variety of bird life, and year after year it was the place I heard larks for the first time, in early Spring . . ."

Invitation to the launch on 2 May 1958 of the Ionic Ferry, sister ship to the Bardic Ferry.

He recalls the period of about 1958-1970 as the heyday of the Preston service.

"There was great pride taken in the maintenance and appearance of these ships. They were a study in polished brass, varnished teakwork, and holystoned decks. The engine rooms were cream paint, brasswork and burnished steel.

"During the summer months the passenger accommodation was invariably booked out and customers certainly got their money's worth. Nothing like it had ever been experienced in cross-channel travel before and certainly not since . . .

"The first and, I think, the only Atlantic Steam Navigation Company vessel to cross the Atlantic was the Cerdic Ferry in 1970 on a charter to run between Nova Scotia and Newfoundland for Canadian National Railways. It gave me great pleasure as Master to send Colonel Bustard a telegram on passing Cape Race informing him that, after so many years, one of his vessels had actually crossed the Atlantic."[12]

In the early Fifties, the ASN Company was taken over by the British Transport Commission as part of the Government's nationalisation policy, but it continued to trade under its own colours as a virtually independent shipping company, although it was part of a

The Bardic Ferry, 3,000 tons, the first of the purpose-built ASN Preston–Larne ferries to replace the older converted tank landing craft (LSTs).

nationalised transport system. By this time the RO/RO revolution was accepted by the major operators, and the ports and routes were firmly established. However, there was a critical need for capital, and under the control of the BTC this much-needed funding became available. During a period of 17 years, six new vessels were built – the Bardic, Ionic, Cerdic, Doric, Gaelic and Europic Ferries, as well as new purpose-built terminals at Felixstowe, and Europort (Rotterdam).[13]

In 1956, the entire ASN fleet was taken over by the Government and used for military service during the Suez crisis, and it was not until January 1957 that normal services were resumed on the North Sea and Irish Sea routes.[14] However, by the beginning of the Sixties the Transport Ferry Service and the Larne-Preston route were well-established. A bullish background briefing from ASN on the Transport Ferry Service (circa 1960) illustrates the confidence of the Company:

"The fleet of The Transport Ferry Service now comprises the two specially built vehicle ferry ships mv "Bardic Ferry" and mv "Ionic Ferry", three LST's, four container ships, and two more vehicle ferries at present under construction. Two LST's (ss "Empire Nordic" and ss "Empire Cymric") and mv "Ionic Ferry" are on the Northern Ireland route, mv "Bardic Ferry" on the Continental route, and one LST (ss "Empire Celtic") is in reserve. The four container ships operate between Preston/Larne and Ardrossan/Larne.

4   *Larne Times, Thursday, July 4, 1957.*

The Editor's Notebook

History-making 'Bardic Ferry'

LARNE BOROUGH COUNCIL, I hear, are to approach their opposite numbers in Preston with a view to presenting plaques of the towns' coats of arms to the new Transport Ferry Service vessel, "Bardic Ferry," in appreciation of the fact that this is the first ship to be specially built by the Service for carrying cargo on the Larne-Preston run.

Preston Council are expected to agree readily enough to the suggestion. In fact, Larne's ex-Mayor, Freeman, Mr. John Girvan, who has been busy carving the town's plaque, has made the journey across to Preston to give them a preview of his handiwork.

The "Bardic Ferry" was launched at Dumbarton last March and is now being fitted out in readiness for "active service" by the end of the summer.

Mr. Ian Duffin, Larne manager of the Transport Ferry Service, tells me she is probably the first cargo vessel to be fitted with Denny-Brown stabilisers and these should make a big difference in the crossing—a case of comfort for the cargo.

Incidentally, master of the new ship is Captain H. T. Green, of Larne, and it is to him that the proposed presentation will be made.

In passing, it is interesting to speculate as to where the presentation will take place—Larne or Preston?

Indeed, we might yet have the opportunity of seeing Alderman Ross and his Preston equivalent donning their sea boots for a ceremony in mid-Channel!

BELFAST NEWS-LETTER WEDNESDAY, AUGUST 28, 1957

New vessel for Larne-Preston service

The Bardic Ferry (3,000 tons), the first of two new vessels for the Atlantic Steam Navigation Company's Preston - Larne service, arriving at Larne Harbour yesterday for berthing trials. The new ships will replace the converted tank landing craft at present in service and will each carry 95 vehicles.

Plaque of Larne coat of arms presented

The Mayor of Larne, Alderman C. Ross, presented last night on behalf of the town the plaque of the coat of arms to the m.v. Bardic Ferry, the latest ship of the fleet on the Larne-Preston ferry service.

The ship, which will commence a regular service between the ports on September 3 will be the sixth of the line, but she is the first to be built specially for the Larne-Preston service. Of 3,000 tons and costing more than £750,000, the Bardic Ferry will carry 95 vehicles as against 60 in the ships now in service. She will also accommodate 55 passengers in two and four-berth cabins.

Among those present at the ceremony were Lt.-Col. Frank Bustard, who inaugurated the service nine years ago, his son, Mr. John Bustard, general manager of the Transport Ferry Service, and Mr. J. L. Harrington, a director and a member of the British Transport Commission, and Mr. James McClenaghan, chairman of Larne Harbour Ltd.

The master of the ship is Captain H. T. Green, Larne.

Mr. John Bustard recalled that the service was started with one vessel, making two calls a week to Larne. Now they had more than a daily sailing. He said that since the service had been inaugurated more than 1,250,000 vehicles had been carried and more than 40,000 passengers.

Presenting the plaques, the Mayor said the town was proud of the achievements of the service, and he paid tribute to the foresight and optimism of Colonel Bustard, who was primarily responsible for the success of the service.

Mr. McClenaghan, who also paid tribute to Colonel Bustard, referred to the fact that a new mail service ship was being built for the Larne-Stranraer service and said the Harbour Company had decided to build a new quay for her.

Replying, Colonel Bustard said it would not be long until the Bardic Ferry was joined by a new sister ship, the Ionic Ferry.

The Bardic Ferry will leave Larne this evening and on its arrival at Preston to-morrow she will be presented with a plaque of the coat of arms of that town.

LARNE TIMES, THURSDAY, MAY 27, 1948.

Captain W. N. Johnson (centre) with (from left) Mr. G. A. Ashley (freight manager), Alderman Squadron-Leader A. Ferris, Mr. C. E. F. Robinson (Mayor of Larne), Mr. J. M. O'Brien, Town Clerk; Mr. D. H. Logan, Harbour Master; Mr. C. N. Barnhill, assistant manager, and Mr. A. Carroll, manager, on board the Empire Cedric after its initial run from Preston.

CROSS-CHANNEL FERRY.

LARNE ARRIVAL.

WITH VARIED CARGO.

The Empire Cedric, 4,000-ton former tank landing ship, arrived at Larne Harbour on Friday morning from Preston to inaugurate the new Irish Sea ferry service. Her cargo included R.A.F. trailers, lorries laden with electric conkers, amphibian "ducks," a new trolley-bus for Belfast Corporation, and several new lorries. There were also a number of cabin passengers and the drivers of the lorries, on board.

When fully laden the ship can carry about 200 motor-cars or between 50 and 60 five-ton lorries. She has cabin accommodation for 12 passengers, and provision is also made for lorry drivers.

The service is operated by the Continental Line, whose managers are Frank Bustard & Sons, Ltd., London. The agents are Thomas Jack & Co., but the firm have a traffic office at Larne Harbour.

Captain W. N. Johnson entertained a number of guests aboard the ship in the afternoon. Among those present were the Mayor of Larne (Alderman C. E. F. Robinson); Alderman Squadron-Leader A. Ferris; Mr. J. M. O'Brien (Town Clerk); Mr. D. H. Logan (Harbour Master); and Mr. R. Mackerell, B.E.M., Station Master at Larne Harbour. The Continental Line were represented by Mr. G. A. Ashley (freight manager), and Mr. A. Carroll and Mr. C. N. Barnhill, local traffic representatives.

Press announcement of the new service

Larne Times, Thursday, August 22, 1957.

'Bardic Ferry' begins era in vehicle transport service

A NEW ERA IN THE FERRY TRANSPORT of vehicles between Preston and Northern Ireland will be inaugurated shortly when the Atlantic Steam Navigation Company, which pioneered the use of drive-on, drive-off vessels, introduce the first ship specially built for vehicle transport.

This is the 3,000-ton Bardic Ferry, built by William Denny and Brothers, of Dumbarton, which is due to leave Greenock on August 26 and will be calling at Larne the following day for berthing trials.

Later the vessel will go to Preston in readiness for her maiden voyage in service on September 2, when one of the passengers will be Mr. John Bustard, director and general manager of the operating company.

The fact that Larne is naming some roads in its new housing estate after ships of the transport ferry fleet indicates a growing sentimental attachment between the borough and the line which is adding so substantially to its commercial importance.

Further evidence of this kind is provided by the fact that Larne is presenting a suitably inscribed replica of its coat of arms to the Bardic Ferry, which will be handed over on August 27 when the Mayor and members of the council are to attend a dinner on board.

A similar gesture is being made by the Borough of Preston, whose presentation is to take place at a luncheon in the ship on Sept. 2.

Equipped with single, two-berth and four-berth cabins to accommodate 55 passengers, including lorry drivers, the Bardic Ferry will be able to carry 95 vehicles as against 60 in the ships now in service. She will bring the number of ferry ships on the Preston-Northern Ireland run to five and next spring will be joined by a sister ship, Ionic Ferry, which is also being built at Dumbarton.

These new ships, diesel driven and capable of 14 knots, compared with 10 knots by the present vessels, will be capable of making six voyages a week and in time they will enable some of the older ships to be transferred to Dublin or Antwerp services.

A notable point is that they are fitted with Denny-Brown stabilisers—employed for the first time for the benefit of cargo and not passengers.

An artist's impression of the Bardic Ferry.

"The Atlantic Steam Navigation Co operate a total of 26 ships. In addition to owning The Transport Ferry Service, the company manages 17 Ministry of Transport ships operating in all parts of the world, including the Mediterranean, Red Sea, Persian Gulf, East Africa and the Far East."[15]

The ASN Company was not backward in putting forward a strong sales pitch, and in underlining its confidence in the future. It stated; "Special advantages of the Service are:-

a.   **Speed.** A road vehicle gives a true door-to-door service, saving time both on the road and at the docks. Approximately 70 vehicles can be unloaded and a further 70 loaded on again within the space of only 3-4 hours.

b.   **No Intermediate Handling.** The elimination of handling means that goods can be delivered direct to the customer. It also avoids damage and pilfering. The goods remain on the vehicle platform throughout the whole journey. The hold is kept locked and is only opened for routine security checks by a ship's officer.

c.   **No Packaging Needed.** Goods shipped by conventional methods often require costly specialised packaging. The necessity for this is greatly reduced when goods remain on their vehicle.

The Future

Each year a large variety of goods cross the Irish Sea and the North Sea via The Transport Ferry Service. Both routes form an important economic link with Northern Ireland and countries on the Continent.

Each year the traffic continues to expand. During 1960 it is estimated that more than half a million vehicles, trailers and containers will have been carried on the Service's routes to Northern Ireland and the Continent."[16]

The new ships for "Transport Ferry Service" were developed from the original LST concept, utilising the same lift-on/lift-off operation for the upper deck with RO/RO on the lower deck through stern openings in the hull. With the growth of the container revolution in the 1950s on a world wide basis, pure Lift-On/Lift-Off (LO/LO) services started in Larne in 1954 and this traffic expanded until around 1970 when there was a gradual return to a purely RO/RO operation.

The return to RO/RO on the Irish Sea was due to the more rapid turn-round of ships and cargo, with consequent cost-savings because of a reduction in the number of handling operations, and reduced risk of damage during these operations. The developments in road transport equipment and improvements to the road system within and outside the province made the transportation of goods more economic and efficient, with increases in the size and weight of loads.

The Bardic Ferry, which was launched on 5 March 1957 and came into service in September, and her sister ship the Ionic Ferry, which began operating in October 1958, were capable of carrying 80-90 vehicles, trailers and containers, and 53 passengers. Fitted with twin-screw diesels, they had a speed of 14 knots. Each was provided with stabilisers to counteract rolling, with the risk of damage to cargo. Vehicles were loaded through a special stern door/ramp.

The Bardic Ferry made her maiden voyage between Preston and Larne on 2 September 1957 and was later transferred to the Tilbury-Antwerp route when the Ionic Ferry became the main vessel on the Preston-Larne service, with two LST's in support. In late 1959, the Empire Cedric was withdrawn from service, and two new vessels were announced. The first of these, named the Cerdic Ferry (slightly confusing to anyone writing about the Empire Cedric) was launched on 16 February 1961 and entered service the following November.

Now that the Transport Ferry Service had four state-of-the-art vessels, the old LST's were withdrawn gradually. By 1963 only the Empire Nordic was in service from Preston, and she was withdrawn from service in 1966. In an era of greater efficiency and cost-effectiveness, the Company found her too expensive to operate. In 1963 the fifth purpose-built vessel, the Gaelic Ferry, was launched, and in 1965, due to increasing demands, the ASN bought the Pima Country, a US tank landing ship. She was renamed the Baltic Ferry and was with the Company for only three years.[17]

In October 1967 the Europic Ferry, the last ASN vessel to be ordered, was launched, and when she began service between Felixstowe and the new Europort in Rotterdam, in January 1968, there was a resultant shuffle of the other vessels.

Meanwhile, major commercial and other factors outside the control of Larne, were leading to two important developments – the ending of the Preston-Larne service, and the acquisition of the war-time,

Cerdic Ferry showing general layout of TFS vessels.

The Stranraer mail steamer Princess Margaret on a day excursion to Ailsa Crag, 1 August 1955.

and hitherto relatively unused port of Cairnryan, which was to have such a dramatic impact on Larne's future. In 1962, the BTC was dissolved, and the ASN's ownership was transferred under the Transport Act to a newly-formed Transport Holding Company. Then in 1968, under yet another Transport Act, the ownership of ASN was transferred to become a subsidiary of a newly-formed National Freight Corporation, though this did not lead to any major changes. However, with the return of a Conservative Government under Edward Heath in 1969, denationalisation was the new received wisdom. The ASN and its subsidiaries became part of European Ferries, better known as Townsend Thoresen, which acquired the goodwill of four routes, seven ferries and three terminals for some £5.5 million.[18]

Meanwhile, the Larne-Preston service had started paying its way by 1952, but navigational difficulties, and a long dock strike in Britain itself in 1969 which damaged its reputation for good labour relations, began to spell out the beginning of the end for the port. The draught restrictions in the Ribble were a problem, and the tidal variance meant that the length and time of the crossing created added difficulties at a period when operators were looking for the maximum utilisation of their vessels. The story of the ASN search for an alternative to Preston is well-documented by Michael Bustard.

"As the months and years busily passed by at Preston, a great opportunity through sheer good luck arose in South West Scotland. It was the then unknown port of Cairnryan, built during

Colonel Frank Bustard whose vision for a new system of moving goods in bulk led to the development of Larne as a major container port. In 1969 he was deservedly given the Freedom of Larne. Colonel Bustard, and James Chaine, almost 100 years previously, were two major figures in the history of the Port of Larne. On the left of the picture is Mrs Mary Logan, wife of David Logan, the manager of Larne Harbour.

the War as No. 2 Military Port. This secret port was used for the loading of ammunition ships for our forces overseas. After the War its only visitor was the occasional vessel dumping ammunition in the North Atlantic; it went to sleep. It was then sold to Mr Pounds, the Portsmouth shipbreaker, who in turn sold it to Queenborough Shipbreakers after disposing of a large number of cranes to the East African Railways.

"In the early Sixties, ASN began secret negotiations with Mr Pounds to acquire part of his Loch Ryan empire. These culminated when the ASN Board, albeit with some well-concealed misgivings, showed great foresight in purchasing 10 acres, known as the Lighterage Wharf, out of Mr Pounds' Scottish estate of 200 acres. Mr Pounds was well satisfied with his sale of a near derelict wharf to a shipping line who were ready to pay £25,000 for waterside land in a remote part of South Western Scotland." (The money was brought to the aptly-named Mr Pounds in a suitcase filled with £50 notes!) Several years were to pass until the new ASN Cairnryan-Larne service was inaugurated by the Ionic Ferry on 10 July 1973. "The effect on ASN's Irish Sea economics was electric. At a stroke the shortest sea crossing between Great Britain and Ireland gave ASN a round voyage ship utilisation of a few hours compared to the previous 48 hours out of Preston. Once again the concept of bridging the ocean at is narrowest point proved unbeatable."[19]

The development of the port of Cairnryan, and the on-going RO/RO revolution, were to have a profound influence on the development of Larne. Colonel Frank Bustard, whose vision had been central to these advances, died in 1973 at the age of 87. He is remembered fondly by his business associates in Larne and elsewhere. Ian Duffin, who was part of the Larne management team for the Transport Ferry Service knew Frank Bustard and recalls: "He was courteous, a real gentleman with a sharp business brain. He was a dapper dresser, and he often wore a dark, greenish suit with a silk pocket handkerchief, and spats. He was a great man for the passengers' comfort, and insisted that everyone would be given two pillows. He wanted the type of service that had been such an attractive part of the White Star line. He had the old "liner" type of style!"

In 1969 Colonel Bustard was given, deservedly, the Freedom of Larne. It is no exaggeration to note, however, that he deserved (and still deserves) a more tangible public memorial, in the way that the work of James Chaine was commemorated. Both men, in different centuries, made contributions to Larne and its citizens which, as subsequent history demonstrated, were beyond measure. They were truly giants in the development of the port.

A Fishy Tale – A large fish washed up on the beach at Brown's Bay, Islandmagee was towed to Larne Harbour where it was removed from the sea by workmen, and then buried in a lime pit in the reclamation area opposite the Olderfleet Hotel. This was part of the development to facilitate the ASN and other services.

1.   "A Study of Carrier Services Between Northern Ireland and Great Britain" by CE Brown, as part of a thesis at Queen's University, Belfast, 1961.
2.   Larne Harbour Ltd Minutes.
3.   Op.Cit p3.
4.   "Across the Irish Sea" by Robert C Sinclair, published by Conway Maritime Press 1990, p124.
5.   Op.Cit p124.
6.   "By Road Across the Sea" by Miles Cowsill, published by Ferry Publications 1990, p20.
7.   Ibid. p21.
8.   Ibid. pp4-5.
9.   Ibid. p7.
10. Ibid. p6-7.
11. Ibid. p21.
12. Ibid. pp24-28.
13. Ibid. p22.
14. The Larne dimension will be covered in Chapter Nine.
15. Archives of Larne Harbour Ltd.
16. Ibid.
17. Op.Cit Miles Cowsill, pp12-15.
18. Ibid pp18-19.
19. Ibid pp22-23.

ON THE MORNING OF 31ST JANUARY 1953 THE M.V. "PRINCESS VICTORIA" LEFT THE EAST PIER STRANRAER, TO MAKE ITS NORMAL CROSSING TO LARNE. OFF CORSEWALL POINT, THE SHIP ENCOUNTERED THE FULL FURY OF THE GALE WHICH WAS THAT DAY TO CAUSE SO MUCH DAMAGE AND LOSS OF LIFE THROUGHOUT THE COUNTRY, AND, DESPITE THE VALIANT EFFORTS OF HER CREW, THE LIFEBOATMEN AND OTHER SEAFARERS, THE "PRINCESS VICTORIA" FOUNDERED OFF THE COAST OF NORTHERN IRELAND WITH THE LOSS OF 133 LIVES. OF THOSE LOST, 27 WERE INHABITANTS OF LARNE, WHOSE DEATH THIS COMMUNITY MOURNS.

The inscription on the Larne memorial to those who died when the Princess Victoria foundered. Picture by Alf McCreary

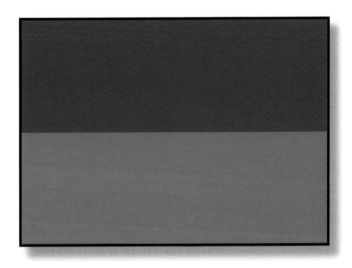

CHAPTER 8

DEVELOPMENT AND DISASTER

The years following the end of the Second World War record the story of the steady development of the port of Larne, with increased services, and also of the horrific sinking of the Princess Victoria which foundered during a fierce storm on 31 January 1953 with appalling loss of life. This was a tragic milestone in the history of Northern Ireland.

This general view of the Port of Larne in the early 1950's shows in the foreground (left) the ramp built in wartime and later used for the Preston–Larne service. Coal was still being landed on the quayside and stored in bins beyond the two sheds in the centre. Further along from the bins is the railway station, and in the Lough (top left), a dredger is working. At the berth is the mail steamer the Princess Margaret. The small vessel to the mid-left is one of the Islandmagee ferries. On the right, opposite the two sheds, is the old Larne Harbour office, to the rear of which is a Post Office and H.M. Customs and Excise office. On the top right are Lobitos oil tanks which were later removed. The crescent-shaped bay in the distance was totally reclaimed for port operations, and the building with a chimney in the far distance was a power station, long since demolished. The two Luffing Cranes on the left were still used occasionally, though located elsewhere in the port, until early in the year 2000.

On 5 November 1945 the Princess Margaret resumed the mail run between Larne and Stranraer, but she returned to the Heysham route when the Princess Maud, after some of her war equipment had been removed, took over until the middle of February 1946. Later the Maud was based permanently at Holyhead. The Margaret then took over the mail run, and the year 1947 became extremely busy-partly because of increased traffic which had been diverted from the Belfast-Heysham service which had been reduced due to a coal shortage.

However, help was on the way, and a new Princess Victoria was ordered from Wm Denny and Bros., Dumbarton for £313,000. This was to be a virtual carbon-copy of the Princess Victoria of 1939, which had struck a German mine in the Humber in 1940 and sank, with the loss of 34 crew.

"Externally, the only difference between the pioneer Stranraer car ferry and her successor was the positioning and shape of certain ventilators. To all intents and purposes they were identical externally,

but internally there was not only a general improvement in the third-class accommodation in both finish and size, but the car-deck did not extend for the full length of the ship. The space forward of the engine casing was given over to cabin and lounge accommodation. The new ship could provide sleeping accommodation for 54; and this included the six cabins on the bridge-deck which had been the only such accommodation on Princess Victoria of 1939. The new "Victoria" could carry a hundred passengers more than her 1939 sister."[1]

Above Left: Princess Victoria carrying milk tankers in 1947 with the black 'guillotine' raised.

Picture courtesy of F. H. McCarlie, Stranraer

Above Right: Tankers driving up the ramp at Stranraer harbour from the Princess Victoria in September, 1949. The ship carried 17 lorries each trip, each holding 1200 gallons.

Her sea trials were carried out on 7 March 1947, and she was scheduled to take over from the Princess Margaret on 17 March, St Patrick's Day, but previously Stranraer had been cut off by a severe snow storm. The Princess Victoria with some 300 passengers on board was forced in a blizzard to anchor off Corsewall Point in the middle of the night, and eventually the ship had to make for Gourock. A fishing boat brought food to the hungry and beleaguered people of Stranraer, and the mail run was abandoned until 18 March, when the new Princess Victoria took over. It was not a happy omen.

The developments on the so-called "milk run" were not encouraging either. This began during the war when milk was transported from Larne to Cairnryan in successive periods by the Irwell, the Hodder and the Felixstowe. In May 1949, the car deck of the Princess Victoria was strengthened, and a spray door, which could be raised or lowered, was fitted to the stern. This allowed the vessel to carry milk tankers, and this was a much more efficient way of transporting milk, compared to handling large numbers of milk churns.[2]

In October 1949 the Princess Victoria was crossing from Larne in heavy weather when some milk tankers broke loose, causing her to list.

She was unable to berth at Stranraer, so while she lay in Loch Ryan, some of the tankers released their milk to reduce the list, thus flooding the deck to a depth of around nine inches. Some fuel also leaked out "and concern was expressed that it required forty minutes for scuppers to clear the deck of this fire hazard."[3] The management were told that larger scuppers were needed to ensure adequate drainage of the car deck, but little or nothing was done. Either the matter was forgotten about, or regarded to have been of no consequence.

Some two years later, another incident concerning the Princess Victoria sounded a further warning about her seaworthiness.

The Princess Victoria set out from Stranraer at 7.45 am on 31 January, 1953 – a day when there were huge storms and exceptionally high seas all across Europe. Later that afternoon she foundered off the Irish coast with the loss of 133 lives.

Picture courtesy of the Larne Historial Society and the Belfast Telegraph

"Princess Victoria left Stranraer at 2330 on Saturday, 24 November 1951, in good weather, but in the early hours of Sunday when running stern-first into Larne Harbour proved difficult to handle. On the second attempt the ship seemed to be setting down on the shore and her acting master, Captain Duckels, swung her round into the strong north-west wind that had sprung up. The "Victoria" encountered a substantial sea, and waves broached her stern doors and a large quantity of water flooded the car deck. Princess Victoria returned to Stranraer with her cargo of empty tankers still on board. It required an hour and a half for the car deck to clear itself of water and the "Victoria" anchored in Loch Ryan at 0530 on the Sunday morning."[4]

Meanwhile, there were other important developments to concentrate the minds of those responsible for running the service. The establishment of the British Transport Commission in 1947 meant the nationalisation of the railways, and the management of the Larne-Stranraer route, which had been carried out by the LM and SR and its local agents, the Caledonian Steam Packet Company, was re-organised in Scotland. By 1952, however, the new "British Railways" had transferred responsibility for Stranraer to London, with a local marine agent attending to "routine matters".

The Board of Larne Harbour Ltd was also turning its attention to the improvement of facilities, and members were considering the construction of a new quay. They asked for Government help, and they discussed the latest offer from Stormont, at a Special Meeting on 7 November 1951. The Ministry of Commerce was prepared to grant one-third of the cost of the extension of the South Pier at an estimated total cost of £300,000, or a sum of £100,000 "whichever is the lesser amount." This offer was conditional upon the first £100,000 of expenditure being met "entirely out of the Company's funds."

The Ministry was also prepared "to consider sympathetically at the appropriate time" an application for a loan under the Development Loans Act (Northern Ireland) 1945, to enable the work to be completed. The question of assistance to other works would be considered in the light of the Company's financial position on the completion of the work at the South Quay. The Board agreed that "before embarking on a scheme of such magnitude, the views of several of the larger shareholders should be obtained."

On 30 November 1951, the Board held another Special Meeting to consider the report of a meeting between representatives of Larne Harbour Ltd and senior civil servants at the Ministry of Commerce three days previously. The Larne representatives said that the offer was not enough. It was difficult, they said, to convince the majority of the Company's Shareholders who were "elderly (over 60 years of age)" that the prospect of higher dividends in 20 years' time was "worth the risk of exhausting all the Company's available reserves." Their bottom line was simple – unless the Government's offer was increased to 50 per cent, there was little hope of the work proceeding.

However, the men from the Ministry were adamant that their offer was not going to be improved. A Mr Strahan, for the Ministry, "reverted to the generosity of the offer made. Leaving aside, for a moment, the importance of Larne Harbour to the Province, which is undoubted, he said that the Company, as a Private Undertaking, was faced with the possibility of the Stranraer Berth collapsing, and the question which should exercise the minds of the shareholders is not one of a possible reduction in dividends, but rather the possibility of the Company being unable to carry out the works." Faced with such plain talk, the Larne representatives said that they would report to their Board, and the meeting ended "in an atmosphere of cordial goodwill." However, the Board was overtaken by events.

There had been strong rumours previously that the mail boat might be transferred from Larne to Belfast. This was fiercely contested at Larne, and the Board had been carrying out a spirited campaign of opposition. However, "the transfer from Larne to Belfast of the

Stranraer steamer was considered by BR desirable on its own merits since, they claimed, 80 per cent of the ship's traffic originated at or was destined for the Ulster capital. An additional daily, all year round, service was to be maintained by Princess Victoria between Stranraer and Larne."[5]

The possibility of such a transfer had the effect of concentrating minds wonderfully on the question of the new extension. The day after the meeting with the Ministry of Commerce officials in Belfast on 27 November, 1951, the Chairman of Larne Harbour Ltd, Mr James McClenaghan, and a fellow Director, Mr HT Browne had a scheduled meeting with British Railways representatives – Captain Perry, Mr Marr and Mr Hollingsworth. Due to the late arrival of the Mail Steamer, ironically, because of bad weather, the meeting was cancelled; but Marr told McClenaghan and Browne privately "that it was most unlikely that the Mail Steamer would be diverted to Belfast provided that suitable facilities are made available at Larne, and if additional accommodation was provided, British Railways had every hope of a sufficient volume of new untapped traffic from Great Britain to justify same."

As a result, the Board members overcame their misgivings about the size of the Government grant on offer, and resolved at the Special Meeting of 30 November, 1951 that "the scheme for a new pier, the plans of which have been approved by the Ministry, be proceeded with, so that the facilities demanded by British Railways will be available."

However, the controversy concerning the possible transfer of the Mail Steamer did not die down, and in May 1952 the Board agreed to send a Director, Major MacKean, and David Logan, the Harbour Manager to "proceed to London and interview responsible officials of British Railways to ascertain what the position is." The matter dragged on and in August 1952, the Company sent a spirited statement to the Ministry of Commerce in support of Larne's claim for the retention of the Mail Steamer service. Copies were also sent to the Mayor of Larne and to the Chairman of Antrim County Council.

The Board stated bluntly that the new pier had to be built in order to retain the Mail Steamer and noted "It is astounding, therefore, to find that when the new pier is actually being erected, British Railways propose to take the service away. This is so illogical and unreasonable that it surely should not be permitted." The Board added "The proposals have the grave disadvantage that they will concentrate even more traffic at Belfast. That would be understandable if it were vital, but with containers, the difference between Larne and Belfast is negligible. We think it is vital to the Province that Larne should continue to be a port of some importance, and the certain way to keep it so is to continue the mail service to it."[6] In December 1952, following a meeting of the Sub Committee of the Municipal Authorities Association, and others, the Board of Larne Harbour Ltd was collating views and preparing its case for presentation in the New Year to the Prime Minister of Northern Ireland and the Minister of Commerce.

No-one could foresee, however, the immense tragedy which was to overshadow any such proposal for the transfer of the Mail Steamer and which would write its own obituary on one of the worst civil tragedies in the history of Northern Ireland. It was also one of the worst disasters to befall British shipping since the loss of the Titanic.

On 31 January 1953, there were huge storms across Western Europe, with hurricane-force winds and exceptionally high seas. There was widespread damage in the United Kingdom. The lighthouse at Margate was washed into the sea, and docks were flooded elsewhere. At Ullapool, 27 fishing-boats were driven onto the shore, and at Immingham a lightship and a cargo ship both capsized as water poured into the graving dock. A state of emergency was declared in the Netherlands, and in northern Belgium. Altogether, eight ships were listed as "missing" in one day by the Committee of Lloyd's, the first time that this had happened in the 20th century.[7]

However, there had been no inkling of the potential intensity of the storm as the highly-respected Captain James Ferguson reported for duty at Stranraer. At 7.45 am he set off to cover the 39 miles to Larne with 127 passengers, 49 crew, and 44 tons of cargo. Everyone was aware that it would not be an easy passage, as high winds had already prevented cars being loaded, and the other cargo had to be loaded by hand – which caused a delay in the vessel's departure. But Captain Ferguson and his senior officers would have been aware of the weather forecast which predicted a moderation in the gale force winds.

On her passage down Loch Ryan, the Princess Victoria passed through squalls of snow and sleet, but visibility was sufficient to allow her to continue the journey, and the hope was that once she hit the open channel, she would be running with the strong seas towards Larne. No-one had anticipated that those same heavy seas would force open her stern doors and lead to disaster.

However, some people believed that she was not a lucky ship, and others felt that her system of drainage for sea water rendered her unsafe. Mrs Hester McGarel, whose husband Archie lost his father on the Princess Victoria, recalled that her own father, a quarter-master on the Larne-Stranraer route, refused to sail on the Victoria because the scuppers, a crucial part of the drainage system, were too narrow.

Soon after the Princess Victoria passed out of Loch Ryan into the open seas, the stern doors were smashed open and buckled by mountainous waves. The second officer and some of the crew tried to jam shut the doors, as the heaving salt-water swirled around them, but to no avail. Captain Ferguson, a most experienced seaman, then turned his vessel head-on into the gale, and it is believed that his intention was to use the bow rudder to make for the safety of Loch Ryan. Because of the heavy seas, and the extremely difficult conditions on board the vessel, it must have proved impossible to release the pin holding the bow-rudder, and this strategy was abandoned.

At 9.46 am, just two hours after leaving Stranraer, the Princess Victoria passed an urgent message to Portpatrick Radio; "Hove to, off mouth of Loch Ryan. Vessel not under command. Urgent assistance of tug required." Unfortunately the only available tugs were marooned by the bad weather in Douglas Bay, Isle of Man. To add to the complications, the manoeuvre to turn the ship head-on into the seas had caused the cargo to shift, and this increased her existing list of 10 degrees to starboard, where there was some five feet of water on the car deck.

Belfast Telegraph

83rd Year.   Monday, February 2, 1953.   Twopence.

65 bodies of Princess Victoria victims so far recovered from the grim

SHIP DISASTER SEARCH IS ABA

OBBING RELATIVES IDENTIFY VICTIMS

Along the coast a watch is kept

THE sea and air search for 65 bodies still missing Victoria was called off to-day as Royal Naval reports that the area was now marked only by empty rafts and wreckage.

Meanwhile pathetic streams of relatives, many of them in tears, made the journey to public, private and hospital mortuaries in Belfast and Newtownards to identify the bodies already recovered.

Brilliant sunshine, calm sea

In brilliant sunshine, and with a calm sea, coastguards, fishermen and police kept watch along the County Down coast for any bodies which might be washed ashore.

Of the 172 people—133 passengers and 49 crew—aboard the Princess Victoria only 44 have survived.

After the loss of the Princess d Air Force chiefs received

Only a few mails were saved

THE PORTMASTER-GENERAL

How the fateful news was reported.

Picture courtesy of the Belfast Telegraph

Buffeted by mighty waves, a lifeboat from the Princess Victoria, filled with life-jacketed figues, fights its way to the tanker Pass of Drumochter.

Picture courtesy of the Larne Times

The service at Larne Harbour Railway Station in commemoration of the victims of the Princess Victoria. Another service was held at Donaghadee.

By 10.30 am sea water was seeping into the lounges and cabins, thus accentuating the sense of grim foreboding. Two minutes later the first SOS was sent by means of Morse code, and within the next sixty minutes life-jackets were issued to passengers and crew. The list to starboard became so bad that lifelines were set up to help passengers pull themselves up towards the port side. As the situation worsened, the lifeboats were prepared for launching. Just before 2.00 pm, the order was given to abandon ship. In the event, six lifeboats and a number of life-rafts were launched, but only 44 people were rescued. No women or children survived. These stark figures in their understated simplicity underline the immensity of the tragedy, and they also disguise the harrowing human stories behind the statistics.

Some eye-witnesses recall a scene where a lifeboat filled mainly with women and children seemed to have had a hope of getting away, but it was dashed against the hull by the massive seas, and the occupants were pitched into the turbulent water. One young man was spotted on a life-raft, but was never seen again. One old lady was unable to move up from below decks, and stayed on to meet her inevitable fate. Another young man clung to a life-raft until he could be hauled on to a nearby lifeboat. It was perhaps no coincidence that the survivors were all young and fit males. The less strong, and the vulnerable, perished.

One survivor saw Captain James Ferguson at the bridge to the very end, when he chose in the traditions of seafaring men, to go down with his ship. The Northern Ireland Minister of Finance and Deputy Prime Minister, Major Maynard Sinclair, was one of the 133 victims.

The memorial at Larne to those who died.

Photo: Alf McCreary

So, too, was Sir Walter Smiles, the MP for North Down. According to one source Smiles "had been left on the ship at his own request. He declared that he was too weak and too ill to leave. Another passenger refused to leave the sinking ship because his dog was still down below in the lounge."[8] The story is told of a woman who gathered small children around her and sang Sunday School choruses with them to try to allay their fears. Yet another survivor talked about being able to see the mouth of Belfast Lough from the upturned ship which eventually went down off the Copeland Islands.[9]

At this remove, it seems almost impossible to believe how all this could have happened. In our modern world of instant communications, helicopter rescue and advanced radar and other navigational aids, such a disaster so close to land would be almost unthinkable. But in the hours of Princess Victoria's great distress, one key factor made the situation worse.

Officers of the Princess Victoria in happier times, during a cruise in 1947. (Left to right) Third Officer, William McInnes, Radio Officer, David Bradford who perished when the vessel sank and was awarded posthumously the George Medal for his bravery, Captain James Ferguson, who went down with his vessel and Chief Officer Shirley Duckels, who also perished.

Due to the lack of advanced radio technology on the Princess Victoria there was no direct communication between the stricken vessel and other ships The Princess Victoria communicated by Morse Code only, but the other vessels used radio to keep in touch with each other and with the Coastguard stations on either side of the channel. Despite the best efforts of the Radio Officer David Broadfoot, who was awarded posthumously the George Medal for his selfless work, the rescue vessels and their crews who heroically battled through the dangerous seas went to the wrong place. "The galling part was the fact that the last message received from the sinking ship was inaccurate regarding her position. HMS Contest, Donaghadee lifeboat, three coasters, a trawler and another lifeboat were proceeding to a position which was nearly five miles too far south and fully one mile too far east of the Princess Victoria's position."[10]

The outstanding heroism on that day was rightly recognised. William McConnell, coxswain of the Portpatrick lifeboat, and Hugh Nelson, coxswain of the Donaghadee lifeboat, were awarded the British Empire Medal, while the George Medal was awarded to Lieut-Commander Stanley McArdle and Chief Petty Officer Wilfred Warren of the destroyer HMS Contest. The MBE was awarded to the Masters of four other vessels which distinguished themselves during the rescue operation Alexander Bell of the Lairdsmoor, David Brewster of Eastcotes, James Kelly of Pass of Drumochter, and Hugh Angus of Orchy.[11]

The subsequent Formal Inquiry concluded that the major causes of the disaster included the inadequacy of the stern doors, and the lack of clearing arrangements for the water which had come on board. The Court blamed the British Transport Commission which was responsible for the ship's safety, and particularly in that it had failed to provide sufficiently strong stern doors, or adequate drainage arrangements for the water on board, and that it failed to take the precautionary steps necessary following the previous mishaps of 1949 and of 1951, already reported. The Inquiry concluded that "if the Princess Victoria had been as staunch as the men who manned her, all would have been well, and this disaster averted."

This was cold comfort, however, for the relatives and for people who had known some of those who had died. Every port has its sad tale of shipwrecks and disasters, but the loss of the Princess Victoria will never be forgotten by the older generation who heard that awful news on 31 January 1953.

1.   "The Short Sea Route" by Fraser G MacHaffie, p141.
2.   Ibid, p143.
3.   Ibid, p144.
4.   Ibid, pp144-145.
5.   Ibid, p146.
6.   Minutes of Larne Harbour Ltd, 20 August 1952, pp81-83.
7.   Op.Cit. Fraser McHaffie, p148.
8.   "Death of the Princess Victoria" by Bill Pollock, Greystone Books 1990, p40.
9.   "Home Truths" BBC Northern Ireland documentary produced by Bruce Batten.
10.   Op.Cit. Pollock, p36.
11.   Op.Cit. MacHaffie, p153.

Archie McGarel

Archie McGarel, who spent 45 years at the Port of Larne.

Mr McGarel is pictured (left) beside the Princess Victoria with Tommy Hunter, a boy porter wearing railway uniform. Tommy later went to sea and at one time was Captain of the Liverpool steamer.

Archie McGarel, who started work at the Port in 1942, joined Larne Harbour Ltd in 1955 as a junior clerk, and retired in 1987 as Secretary and a Director of the Company. During his 45 years at the Port he saw many major improvements, and he met a host of interesting characters. But the most searing memory of all was the sinking of the Princess Victoria in which his father died. He recalls the tragedy and its aftermath.

"My father William was not a seafaring man. He had been in the Army and was wounded at the Battle of the Somme. As a result he was never in the best of health, and had to take a series of light jobs in civvy street. However he was enouraged by Davy Logan, the Manager of Larne Harbour Ltd., and Norman Canning, a member of one of the coal-importing families, to take a job on the ferry. Within a few months the Princess Victoria tragedy occurred.

"We knew that the vessel had left Stranraer and we heard on BBC Radio that she was in the middle of a very bad storm. However, I said to my mother "Don't worry, nothing ever happens to big boats like this."I was wrong, and the Princess Victora went down about five miles off the Copeland Islands. We were all stunned. I found it hard to take in, because these boats had been coming and going in all weathers, and I never felt that they would ever be in real trouble."

Archie had the sombre task of identifying his father's body, among those of many other of the victims. Initially he was directed to a hall in Newtownards, to which a number had been brought, but he could not find his father's remains there. Then he went to Belfast. "They took me into a room and there were quite a lot of bodies laid out, all the way beside a big, long wall. There were Service people, including Wrens, and a woman in a fur coat.

"One man I knew had his face twisted, as if he had lost his false teeth. It's strange the things you remember. I spotted my father right at the very end of a row. I recognised him by the clothes he was wearing. I was not surprised, for I had expected the worst, but there was a kind of numbness. I returned home and phoned the undertaker in the middle of the night, and told him where to find my father's body. He was taken home, and buried a couple of days later. The shock lasted for a very long time afterwards."

William McGarel was 55 when he died, and he left a grown-up family of three boys and two girls. Archie, the eldest, further recalls "My mother Annie Jane never really got over it. She used to go out with my father quite a bit, but she never had the same zest for life again. For six months I did not go out anywhere myself. I went to work and stayed at home with my mother in the evenings. It was a depressing time, and it was very hard to accept. I just felt that nothing like that could ever happen to people on those big boats."

Archie's father-in-law David Robinson, a quartermaster on the Larne ferries. He was later a bosun on the Princess Margaret, and a friend of Captain James Ferguson, Master of the Princess Victoria.

Archie and Hester McGarel at their home in Islandmagee.

Personal effects found in the clothes of William McGarel, who died in the Princess Victoria disaster. Significantly, the pocket watch is stopped at approximately 2:13, the time when the vessel was in her last throes. The presence of the small pebble would suggest that it may have been caught up in the deceased's clothing whilst in the water. These belongings were kindly made available by Mr McGarel's nephew

Photo: Alf McCreary

NORTH ATLANTIC DRIFT

0 TO 20 MILES PER DAY

quarter and often stormy

...om a westerly

NW

330

320

NWbW

310

300

WNW

290

280

WbN

270

W

260

250

WSW

240

SWbW

230

SW

220

SWbS

210

SSW

200

SbW

190

S

180

SbE

170

SSE

160

SEbS

150

SE

140

SEbE

130

ESE

120

EbS

110

E

100

90

EbN

80

ENE

70

NEbE

60

NE

50

NEbN

Water

Dingle B.

Cork

Bantry B.

C. Clear

C. Finisterre

Vigo B.

Co

Opo

LISBO

C. St Vincent

Gibra

PORTUGAL CURRENT

0 TO 25 MILES PER DAY

In Summer the weather is
normally fine with moderate
winds usually from a northerly
quarter. In winter the weather
is unsettled but seldom stormy

Flores

Corvo

Graciosa

San Jorge

Fayal

San Miguel

AZORES

Formigas

Sta Maria

Mag. Varⁿ 20° W.

Mag. Varⁿ 15° W.

The navigational chart used on Captain
Close's lifeboat after his vessel was
torpedoed.

Porto Santo

Madeira

Dezerta Grande

C. Blanco

Safi

Mogador

Agadir

Salvages

Lanzarote

CANARY Is

Palma

Tenerife

Fuerte
ventura

Gomera

Ferro

Gran Canaria

C. Juby

at times

22° W.

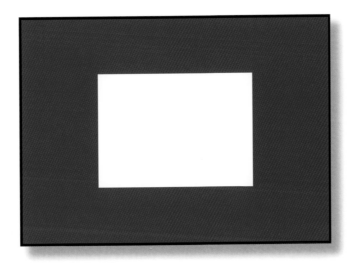

CHAPTER 9

A SEAFARING TRADITION

One of the great traditions of Larne port has been the courage and skills of its seafarers. Many rose through the ranks to take command of vessels, and served with distinction in many parts of the world. Most could recall fascinating tales of experiences in exotic places. In mid-life many of them settled down to a seafaring life based in Larne, often for domestic reasons, and they spent their mature years as senior officers and finally Captains on the cross-channel ferries.

Captain William Close whose vessel was torpedoed in the North Atlantic during World War II. He survived a ten-day ordeal in a lifeboat before being rescued by HMS Londonderry. Captain Close is holding one of the rowlocks which he brought with him from the lifeboat. In the background is a bone model of an early 19th Century Ship-of-the-Line made by a French prisoner-of-war, and restored by Captain Close.

Photo: Ivan Ewart

Such a man is Captain William Close, now over 80 and one of the best-known and most highly-respected mariners from Larne. He is a modest man, and his almost laconic account of his career tends to underplay the early excitement and adventures of a long life at sea. Like so many mariners, a sea-faring tradition ran in the family, and his great-grandfather and two of his uncles were seafarers.

He left Larne Grammar School at 16. He says "I had no desire to stay at school. I was fascinated by shipping and curious about foreign lands." He applied for a Deck Officer's apprenticeship to Alfred Holt and Company, of Liverpool, who ran the Blue Funnel Line. Following an interview, he was accepted on the satisfactory completion of his school year. (It was noted during this interview that an uncle had served with the Blue Funnel Line in the years prior to the First World War.) Before embarking on his first voyage, the young William Close was required to equip himself (at his parents' expense) with the necessary clothing for a voyage that would take him to the Far East. This included a uniform, shoes, boots, dungarees and oilskins, all to a cost of approximately £30 – which was quite a sum in the Mid-Thirties.

Much later, in the summer of 1991, Captain Close wrote about his experiences in The Corran, the Journal of the Larne and District Folklore Society. He described in detail his feelings of apprehension and excitement in those early days, when he received a letter from the Blue Funnel Line asking him to report for duty:

"Also enclosed was my Apprentice's Indenture, a very legal sort of document printed on linen, on which was set out my obligations and entitlements in somewhat archaic language. For example 'The said William Close voluntarily binds himself Apprentice unto the said Alfred Holt and Company for the term of 4 years from the date hereof,' and 'the said Apprentice will not frequent Alehouses or Taverns, unless upon the business of the said Masters', 'the said Masters hereby covenant with the said Apprentice that during the said term they, the

A copy of Captain Close's Apprentice's Indenture – "A very legal document printed on linen".

said Masters, will and shall use all proper means to teach the said Apprentice the business of a seaman.'

'The Masters agree to provide the said Apprentice with sufficient Meat, Drink, Lodging, Medicine, and Medical and Surgical Assistance, and to pay the said Apprentice the sum of £60 in the manner following, that is £6 for the first year, £12 for the second, £18 for the 3rd, £24 for the 4th year'." My father signed the document as my Surety, and our family Doctor, William J Wilson, witnessed both our signatures."

"In due course the clothing and the gear which had been ordered at my parents' expense was delivered to my home, and the sight of it opened out filled me with feelings of anticipation mixed with trepidation. On the evening of 6 July (1936), I said farewell to my parents on Donegall Quay in Belfast, and when I went aboard the Liverpool boat weighed down by my trunk and a seabag, I knew that I would not see them or my friends for several months, and I felt very much on my own amongst strangers."

At that stage he was still not yet 17. Later in the same edition of The Corran he described his first voyage:

"For the first couple of days it was a case of finding one's own way around the ship and keeping one's eyes and ears open. Once at sea we were not idle though, for there was a lot of washing-down to be done, after the period spent in port discharging and loading. The ship had been built in 1905 and was a coal-burner, and since she had been recently bunkered, there was coal-dust everywhere.

" . . . After ten days, the ship reached Port Said where she moored to buoys, awaiting transit through the Suez canal. Here I experienced for the first time the sights and smells of the East, and the gabble and jabber of the Bum Boat men who scrambled aboard trying to sell everything from bars of soap to saddles for camels. 'Dirty' postcards were prominent amongst their wares. Here too the first mail from home was received and eagerly read.

"That was the routine procedure which continued throughout the five months the voyage lasted. The ship discharged at Penang, Port Swettenham, Singapore, Hong Kong and various ports to Japan, and she re-loaded in the reverse order, more or less. Outward bound she carried heavy machinery, Singer Sewing machines and manufactured goods such as cigarettes and cotton garments etc. Homeward bound, the cargo was made up of silk from Japan, cases of mandarin oranges and pineapples, rice, barrels of ginger and drums of essential oils, latex, sheet rubber and ingots of tin . . . all very exotic products in my young mind.

"When I stepped ashore in Liverpool in late November, I was eagerly looking forward to ten days leave at home. I remember the luxury of my first proper bath after washing out of a bucket for 5 months, and after sharing a small room with 3 other big fellows. The days passed all too quickly, but at least when I was recalled to join my next ship I had a good idea of what to expect, and was prepared for it."

He had embarked on a career which would have fascinated any young man of 16, with deep-sea voyages to the Far East and Australia, and back again. Some of the journeys took between four and five months at a time. Captain Close recalls "We served very long hours, but the food on the Blue Funnel ships was good, partly because we had refrigerators even in those days. The food on some of the other ships was indifferent in quality and quantity."

In a time of limited air travel, the transporting of pilgrims to Mecca was carried out by sea, a tradition dating back many centuries. "We brought them mostly from Singapore to Jeddah, and the journey took about two weeks. Up to 1,200 were carried in the tween decks, and these were cleaned out and whitewashed before the pilgrims came on board. They slept on deck mats or simple camp beds, and they hung curtains across their quarters for privacy. No single women were allowed on board."

Sheep and goats were carried live, slaughtered on board and cooked over wood fires resembling large barbecues. With such large numbers, the supply of all fresh water was carefully controlled, and issued twice daily only.

This exotic "cargo" was generally well-behaved, and Captain Close recalls that there was "no real trouble." He says "I also remember that pointers indicating the direction of Mecca had to be adjusted according to the ship's progress, so that the pilgrims were always able to pray while facing in the right direction!"

In 1940 Captain Close, following examination, qualified for his Second Mate's ticket, for which he had studied in Belfast, and he took up the post of Third Mate on a vessel bound for West Africa. Captained by an Islandmagee man, it was making for Freetown, and set off in a large convoy, as was the custom in war-time. However, the vessel developed boiler trouble, lost its place in the convoy and had to set off alone for the Azores.

It waited there for approximately four months while repairs were carried out, and once again set out for its destination. But two days out of the Azores, it was torpedoed by an Italian submarine. Captain Close takes up the story "All the crew got off, except for two men. One fell down a hatch and the other was killed in the engine-room where the torpedo struck. The rest of us ended up in two lifeboats. Ours had 21 men, but two died, including one who lost his mind and jumped overboard. We spent nine or ten days rowing and under sail, trying to make our way back to the Azores. Conditions were tough, and we lived on special lifeboat biscuits (a bit like dog biscuits), with our ration of water and condensed milk. I had a raging thirst, and I would have given my right arm for a drink."

"After ten days or so, the situation was very difficult and we knew that if we had to spend another ten days at sea the conditions would have been desperate. However, help was at hand. I was in charge of the lifeboat at that time and on seeing a vague shape of a ship in the distance, I lit a hand-held flare. The vessel came quickly to our rescue, and it turned out to be the sloop HMS Londonderry, which had been escorting an outward bound convoy. When she hove to, there was a great sense of relief. They brought us on board and gave us food and medical treatment. In due course we were transferred to another ship in the convoy, and we eventually reached Freetown."

A blockade ship in Port Said during the 'Suez Canal Crisis'.

Loading vehicles at Malta prior to the Suez invasion.

Captain Close, then only 22, was given home leave, but he barely mentioned his adventure to his parents. Shortly afterwards he returned to sea and served throughout the war, with all its considerable dangers for merchant shipping. This included voyages to the Middle East to bring supplies to the Allied forces for the Desert War, and also to New Zealand and Australia, returning by way of the Panama Canal. Because of enemy action, the Blue Funnel Line lost some 40 vessels, which was practically half of their ships. Captain Close, with remarkable understatement, describes his own journeys during those perilous days as "relatively uneventful."

After the war he continued to serve with the Blue Funnel Line. During this period there were two important developments in his life – he passed the examination for Master, and he married his wife Maureen, a local girl who was later to become a co-founder of The Corran. After his marriage he undertook four more extended voyages with the Blue Funnel Line, but the home roots were tugging and he left the deep seas to join the Irish Lights Commissioners as an officer in the vessels taking supplies to lighthouses and also maintaining buoys around the Irish coast.

However, in 1949 a great opportunity arose to combine a career in the cross-channel ferry service, while maintaining his home base at Larne. He took up a post with the the new Transport Ferry Service, and joined the Empire Cedric and later the Empire Gaelic, where he remained until he was promoted Master of the Empire Doric in 1954. Nevertheless, it was not all plain sailing, and in 1956 vessels of the Transport Ferry Service were requisitioned by the Government during the Suez Canal crisis.

Captain Close took part in this operation and recalls being involved in a convoy of 15 to 20 ships, arriving in Port Said after a five day journey from Malta which involved nightly black-outs. However a cease-fire was declared before any of the LST vessels were able to enter the Port. Captain Close recalls "There was no opposition, and little danger involved, but several burning buildings and columns of smoke created the classic invasion background." Characteristically he describes the whole operation thus "Although this episode certainly had its element of variety and interest, one remembers it as a period of confusion and frustration." He felt that it had been an ill-starred enterprise.

After Suez, Captain Close returned to the Larne-Preston run and served in various vessels, including 13 years as Master of the Ionic Ferry. In March 1973 the Larne-Preston service closed, and until his retirement in 1984 he was Master at various times on all the vessels on the Larne-Cairnryan route, and made the inaugural crossing – from Larne to Cairnryan – in 1973 on the Ionic Ferry. For the next 11 years he served mostly on the Free Enterprise IV, and latterly on the Europic Ferry.

Even in his retirement his heart is still very much with the sea, and from his home on the seafront at Larne Harbour he can maintain an interest in all things nautical. He is at heart a philosopher with a wealth of experience of the sea in all its moods.

The Empire Doric, under the command of Captain William Close, leaving Larne en route to Preston. The picture also shows, in the foreground, warehouses and trailers at the North End, and construction of an extension to the Pye Radio works.

"The job was never boring, because the conditions were always different. You were conscious of the varying moods of the sea which made you treat it with the utmost respect at all times. When deep-sea we navigated by celestial bodies as had been the practice since about the mid-18th century, when the chronometer had been perfected by John Harrison. We were aware of the immensity of the Universe, but now it's all done by computers and satellites, and that is bound to erode people's regard for Nature.

"I have many wonderful memories, including as a young man sailing down the Red Sea and seeing Mount Sinai in the distance, in those days approached by camel tracks. Few people from Larne at my age would have set eyes on these almost legendary locations. Looking back, I would not have done anything different. I am most grateful that I had such a fulfilling career."

Tommy Shields, a Larne man with a remarkable story of war time adventures, with his wife Jeannie.

Photo: Ivan Ewart

Some Larne seafarers have stories of adventure which are almost stranger than fiction, and the matter-of-fact way in which they play down their exploits only adds to the sense of drama. For example, Tommy Shields, who was born in Larne in 1918, was shipwrecked more than once, taken prisoner of war, called up for the Korean War, and served during the Suez Crisis. In his own quiet way he was an integral part of history in the making.

He joined the Royal Navy when he was still under 17, and served on the the battleship HMS Rodney. He was a crew member in various vessels, and eventually served in the Mediterranean on a destroyer, the HMS Gurkha, which patrolled the Mediterranean Coast during the Spanish Civil War. He says "Our role was to maintain the blockade and to try to stop supplies getting to the forces in Southern Spain. I remember a man called "Potato" Jones, who was Master of a Welsh tramp vessel which was trying to smuggle in spuds. He was stopped a few times but we could not arrest him because he was outside the three-mile limit off the Spanish Coast! I also remember being in the port of Almeria when a German battleship was dive-bombed by Spanish planes, and 17 seamen were killed. This caused an international incident."

During the Second World War, Tommy was still serving on the HMS Gurkha which was patrolling off the Norwegian coast when it was located by German aircraft and crippled by a direct hit amidships. He recalls "The ship was sinking slowly, and I was one of the last to get off because I was still one of the men firing our guns at the German planes. Eventually I had to go into the sea, but it was not too difficult because the ship was up on one end and I slid down to the water on a rope."

"It was very cold and there was a mixture of oil and salt-water. Not being a very good swimmer, I stayed afloat doing a 'dog-paddle', but luckily we were picked up quickly by rescue vessels and taken to sick-bay. The next day we were visited by an Admiral who told us 'Those who are ill can stay in sick-bay, and those who are feeling better can go home on leave.' So I got better very quickly."

Tommy returned home on a week's leave, and being the first Larne man to have been shipwrecked during the war, he was given a hero's welcome. "They presented me with a silver watch, a Bible and War Bonds, and I am sure that many a Larne man wanted to be shipwrecked after me! My Bible later became all soggy and dog-eared, but that is another story. I had it with me when I was shipwrecked again, this time when our motor torpedo boat was sunk off the coast of Crete."

For a few days, he and another Ulsterman lived off the land, sleeping rough and foraging for food, but eventually they were captured by the Germans. Tommy ended up in a camp for Irish prisoners near Berlin. "The conditions were very bad. I had never let on that I was in the Royal Navy, but when a new batch of prisoners were being checked in, I sneaked onto the end of the line and told them that I was a Royal Navy man."

Foredeck view of HMS Gurkha, a tribal class destroyer, which was sunk by German aircraft off Norway on 9th April, 1940. Tommy Shields was on board.

As a result, he was transferred to a prisoner-of-war camp at Mulburg and then to another camp near Bremen, where the conditions were much better. After a while he was taken to a work-camp in the Harz Mountains where the conditions further improved. "At night I used to nip out past the old German guards to keep a date with a German girl I had met, called Gisela. We used to go to a local park and when anyone came past she would give the Nazi salute and say 'Heil Hitler'. I was very nervous but she thought it was great 'crack'."

Tommy and Gisela became close friends, and towards the end of the war, she hid him in her home, with her parents' assistance. He recalls "One night I heard what I took to be the Allies at the point of liberating the town, and I rushed into the street shouting 'Thank God they've come'. But I discovered that it was only thunder and lightning. I was amused to find out that several other blokes on the same caper as me had done the same!"

When the war ended, Tommy Shields made his way back home through France by using all kinds of improvised transport, and he lost touch with Gisela and her family. For a while he worked

Tommy Shields and a German wartime friend Gisela.

in 'civvy' street, as a bread-server on a local horse-drawn cart. However, he was not destined to be a businessman, partly because he was too soft on bad debts, and he returned to sea.

He joined the Transport Ferry Company and for several years he worked as a bosun. When the Company's ships were requisitioned for service during the Suez Crisis, he sailed with Captain Close to Port Said. He says "We arrived a bit late for the action but it was one heck of a contrast to life on the Larne-Preston crossing!"

After Suez he returned to normality and later he joined the cruise liners. "I was a physical education instructor, and one of my roles was to devise entertainment for the passengers and keep them occupied. By this time my first marriage had ended in divorce, and I met Jeannie, the girl who became my second wife. Eventually I left the sea, and settled down to shore life in England, where I had a job in Regent Street Post Office in London."

Tommy and Jeannie were inveterate travellers and on one journey in what was then Communist Germany, they found themselves not far from the village where he had been held as a prisoner of war. "Jeannie suggested that I look it up again, so we crossed through the border check-point, and sure enough we found the place where I had been kept. It looked different, but I had no doubt that I was in the right place."

His wife suggested that they try to find the house where his former girl-friend Gisela had lived. "We searched around for a bit, and then I found it. So I knocked on the door, and, would you believe, it was opened by Gisela's mother. She looked at me and said, straight out, "Paddy, how are you!" I could hardly believe it. She told me, to my surprise and delight, that Gisela was alive, and married to an American Air Force Colonel, living in El Paso, Texas."

Tommy and Jeannie returned to England and settled into their normal working routine, after their holiday. Tommy then takes up the story "One day I was behind the counter, and lo and behold, who walks in but Gisela and asks 'How are you Tommy?'. That was the beginning of a new friendship, and we stayed in touch for many years until she died in 1998. It was a remarkable story, and some people do not believe me, but it really happened!"

In later life Tommy returned to live in Larne, with Jeannie, but even after a lifetime of travelling he was still capable in his late Seventies of setting off to drive to Italy in a camper! His story would provide the basis for a gripping novel.

Another seafarer with a fascinating story was Captain Eric Pollock who, in the classical tradition, started his career as a deep-sea voyager in the Far East and later transferred to the Larne -Stranraer route. Sadly, he died in April, 1999. He was a man with many memories of seafaring characters and the vessels in which they sailed.

He was born in Airdrie into a family of engineers, but two uncles went to sea, one on the deep sea routes and the other on the Larne-Stranraer crossing, and he followed their example. In 1935 he joined the Head Line as a "midshipman", with a six-months contract, and he had to pay a £50 premium for the privilege of doing so! After learning the ropes of his new profession – almost literally – he went to Nautical School to study navigation, and secured a job with the Anglo-Saxon Petroleum Company whose vessels sailed world-wide.

Some two years before his death, he recalled in an interview "My first job provided splendid training, with largely British officers and a Chinese crew. I was able to go up to the bridge a lot, but after every voyage I was quickly brought down to earth by having to clean the tanks after discharge! We were based in London, but we went everywhere – to Curacao, the Americas, the Gulf, Singapore, Japan, in fact all over the globe. It was a wonderful experience for a young man".

The late Captain Eric Pollock, a seafarer who had many adventures – "If you spend a lifetime at sea, you develop a respect for deeper things."

Captain Pollock was not one to miss a good anecdote. "On one of our voyages in the Far East, a Chinese member of the crew died, and we had to bury him at sea. I was good at sewing, and it was my job to make the canvas shroud. So I sewed it up, but where do you think I put the last stitch with the long crooked needle? It was through the man's nose – just to make sure that he had really died!"

During the Second World War, Captain Pollock had more than his share of drama. A vessel on which he was a member of the crew was carrying aviation fuel when it was torpedoed by a German submarine in the mid-Atlantic, with loss of life. He said "We could not swim away fast enough from the burning fuel, and a number of men were trapped in the flames. We could do nothing to help, and it was terrible to hear their screams."

On another occasion he was an officer on a ship which was mined in the North Sea. "The vessel was beached, but the bow was not too badly damaged, and we were able to limp back to London. It was a terrible feeling for all of us. The Captain was badly hurt, and died later from spinal injuries."

Captain Pollock, pictured in retirement.
"There were many fine people who have
sailed into and out of Larne."

Photo: Ivan Ewart

During the war Captain Pollock married a Bangor girl, and their story is reminiscent of the atmosphere of those uncertain times. "My ship was in Middlesborough and my girl-friend, a Red Cross nurse, had flown over with a patient. She said to me 'I have had a wedding-ring made', and I replied 'We might as well get married now', so we sought the help of a Canon from the local cathedral. I was married before I was a Master!"

After the war Captain Pollock decided not to go back to deep-sea voyaging because "a wife who is married to a deep-sea Captain is, in effect, a widow with a husband alive." Instead he decided to put down roots at Ballygally in a house built by his wife's grandfather, and after service on various crossings between Britain and Ireland, he secured a job on the Larne-Stranraer route. "Like most deep sea mariners I was happy to 'come ashore'. I had seen the world."

He sailed regularly with the Princess Victoria, and was Chief Officer on the vessel up to a month before she was lost. Like so many others, he felt the loss keenly because many of those who died had been his former colleagues and friends. He said "Strangely enough, the Princess Victoria was a lovely ship to sail in, but there is no doubt that the scuppers were not big enough to drain away the water even under fairly normal conditions."

Captain Pollock, like every Master on the regular crossings, had his own difficulties, despite his long experience of all kinds of weather. He told the story of one particularly complex berthing episode at Larne which reveals that despite all the technological aids of the day, in times of trouble the skills of the Captain and senior officers are still of paramount importance.

"I remember one night when I was bringing in the Caledonian Princess to Larne, it was very difficult, with a strong westerly gale. We were due to berth at 5pm, and to get away at 7pm, but we had lost some time on the crossing. We came into Larne stern-first but just as I was bringing her in to berth, she was caught by a strong gust of wind and blown away from the dockside. I went round again and tried to bring her in bow-first, which no-one did in those days, but she was blown off by the gale yet again.

"After several attempts I brought her round and using the wind I managed to get her berthed. I was so busy that I did not feel the tension, but it was only afterwards that I realised the strain I had been under. If I had been unlucky and had beached her, that would probably have been the end of my career. Being Master of a ship was always a doubtful honour! I was told later that people in the Olderfleet Bar had been watching the drama and someone had said 'Don't worry, it's Captain Pollock on the bridge – he'll get her in'."

Despite the occasional drama, there was also time for humour, and many of the Captains were great characters as well as accomplished sailors. Captain Pollock recalled:

"One real character was Captain Joseph Unsworth, who looked a bit like Sir Alec Guinness. He was a great practical joker, and one of his tricks was to tie a kipper on the manifold of my car to create a stink. He professed to be an atheist, but if the weather was very bad he would start chewing the corner of his handkerchief. If the situation worsened he would begin to hum a hymn tune, and if it was becoming desperate you could hear him up on the bridge singing to himself 'Nearer my God to Thee!'."

Captain Pollock was not without his own brand of humour. "I enjoyed my life at sea, but I would have been happier as a scrap merchant, where you could make lots of money! Seriously, however, it was a wonderful experience to have sailed all over the world and to have met so many fascinating people. My time as a seafarer taught me to have a high regard for Nature, and never to meddle with the sea, because it can be very much a cruel sea. ''

"It also gave me a sense of the religious side of life, and if I was still able to do so physically, I would go to church regularly. Some people treat God like a solicitor, and consult Him only when they are in trouble, but I am not like that. If you spend a lifetime at sea, you develop a respect for the deeper things, and also a high regard for the skill, loyalty and courage of your colleagues. There were, and are, many fine people who have sailed into and out of Larne, and it has been a privilege to have known them."

A sketch by the artist Raymond Piper of the "Caledonian Princess" loading at Larne Harbour circa 1962.

An aerial view of the port in 1966 shortly after Larne Harbour Ltd. bought 70 acres of the "Sloblands" for £6000.

Photo: Arthur Winter, Preston

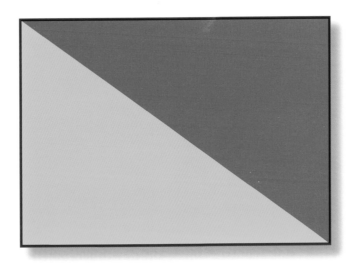

CHAPTER 10

TOWARDS THE MODERN AGE

The decades from the early Fifties to the early Seventies witnessed the development of key facilities to equip Larne fully for its role as a modern port. The mail and passenger service remained important, but with the rapid growth of containerised traffic, the Port's main function developed as a major link between the transport systems on either side of the Irish Sea. Consequently Larne had to organise its operations so that delays were avoided as far as possible and that loads were handled efficiently and economically.

The physical developments were matched by new management initiatives, including the implementation of a pension scheme, productivity agreements and other measures to bring an essentially locally-owned Company into a new era of business practice. These developments, as well as the changing patterns of cross-channel commercial and passenger traffic, made considerable demands on the Board and the harbour staff. Throughout this period, however, while symbolically the world of pen and ink and of high-stools and ledgers began to make way for computers and work-stations, the daily business at the Harbour retained its somewhat paternal and friendly atmosphere. But by 1973 when European Ferries took over, a new order was on the way.

One of the most striking developments of the period was the proliferation of new quays and of loading and unloading facilities, and the Board showed vision in developing the facilities needed. In the decade from 1955, several new quays were constructed, an existing one was extended, and extensive land reclamation was carried out.

The arrival of the first of the concrete (Mulberry) Caissons at Larne Harbour on 24th May, 1952, to be incorporated in the construction of the South Quay Extension. The Caissons were designed for use as temporary harbours for the invasion of France in June, 1944.

The Olderfleet Quay which had been reconstructed in 1942 was extended in 1955. The Phoenix and Curran Quays were built in 1956, and formally opened by the then Governor of Northern Ireland Lord Wakehurst. The Castle Quay was constructed between 1961-62.

OPENING OF PHEONIX AND CURRAN QUAYS ON 10 MAY 1956

1.

2.

4.

3.

1. Lord Wakehurst, (right) the Governor of Northern Ireland in 1956 greets harbour employees: (left to right) George Bryson, Berthing Master; Foreman Stevedore Billy Hart, a former RSM, and Andy McIlrath, the Foreman Fitter.

2. The same picture from a different angle. On the extreme right David Logan, the Harbour Manager, has a word with Chairman James McClenaghan, complete with old-style hearing aid. In the background is the photographer, complete with Fifties-style trilby, trench-coat and ancient camera.

3. Lord Wakehurst unveils the plaque.

4. A general view of the ceremony. In the background are the official cars and the marquee for the celebrations. In the middle-ground (right) a mother and child watch history being made, complete with old-fashioned pram.

Photos: J & S.M. Browne, Larne

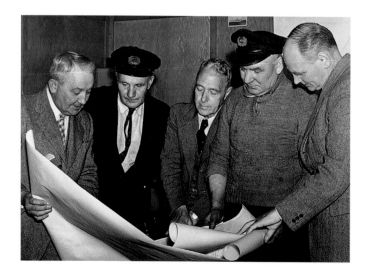

The two Tug Skippers showing officials of Larne Harbour Ltd. the route they took with the Caisson. From left: DH Logan, Harbour Manager; Henry McKenzie, Skipper; HT Browne, Director; Tom McKeague, Skipper and J McClenaghan, Chairman.

Photo: Belfast Telegraph

A significant feature of the Phoenix and Curran Quays was the use of Mulberry Harbours which had been built to provide logistic support for the Allied invasion of Normandy, and a number of these ex-Service structures were purchased in Scotland for use at Larne. The shortage of steel piling after the end of the Second World War meant that other materials had to be incorporated to minimise its use. However, the extra problems and costs involved in using these alternatives were considerable, and it was found later on that measures had to be taken to prevent excessive movements of the Mulberrys supporting the quays, due to scour (erosion) from ships' propellers which undermined the Mulberry caissons.

By the early Sixties, one outside observer was able to report the considerable progress that was being made at Larne Harbour. RF Lambert, writing in the June 1963 edition of "The Dock and Harbour Authority" magazine noted that "The port now has eight quays varying in length from 300 to 400 feet, with a total length of 2,600 feet, and a low-water depth between 15 and 19 feet. Five of these are normally used for container and vehicular traffic, three being equipped with 15-ton and two with 25-ton electric derrick cranes. Two of these berths have ramps for the roll-on roll-off vehicle and car service."

The significant increase in trade and also the number of vehicles passing through the port was underlined by the statistics in Lambert's report. Between 1954 and 1962 the total export and import cargo rose from 385,000 tons to 773,000 tons. The total number of vehicles passing through Larne increased from 3786 in 1948 to 71006 in 1962. During the same period, the number of ships using the port rose from 758 to 1931. There was an even more dramatic increase in the number of containers passing through Larne. It rose from 4077 in 1955, the first full-year of operation, to 36,532 in 1962.

Lambert noted that "These impressive results were not obtained without effort. The system requires sufficient accommodation to allow ships to berth without delay and so make full use of the quick turn-around offered. Lorries and other vehicles must have ample space to enable them to come alongside or actually drive on board without congestion. Space is required also for parking a large number of trailers and containers. The general layout, in fact, must be designed especially for this type of traffic." Although Lambert's comments today seem blindingly obvious, he was outlining what any major port had to do to keep abreast of developments, and this is precisely what Larne was about.

The initiative of the Larne Board paid dividends. As has been noted in Chapter Seven, pure specialised lift-on/lift-off services started in Larne in 1954, and this type of traffic expanded until around 1970, when there was a gradual return to a purely RO/RO (roll-on/roll-off) operation, for reasons referred to earlier.

The Transport Ferry Service increased its commitment to Larne and on 2 September 1956, it began a LO/LO (lift-on/lift-off) service to Ardrossan, while Northern Ireland Trailers Ltd inaugurated its LO/LO services between Larne and Preston and Ardrossan on 27 August 1956. Anglo-Continental Container Services Ltd initially used Transport Ferry Service vessels on the Preston route, but later developed their own services between Larne and Ardrossan in the mid-Fifties, using chartered Dutch vessels.

In April 1972, the Preston RO/RO service was reduced to three sailings per week, and was discontinued on 25 March 1973. However Ferrymasters began an historic association with Larne by starting a Fleetweed LO/LO service only a month later, on 25 April. In July of the same year, Transport Ferry Service started its RO/RO service between Larne and Cairnryan, thus opening up another significant new chapter in the history of this route.

It soon became clear that a modern passenger terminal would be needed to replace the existing wooden station. This matter occupied a good deal of the time and effort of the Larne Board, judging by the voluminous amount of correspondence with Government agencies and other bodies, which was reported in the Minutes. The report of a meeting on 19 May 1966 between the Board and representatives of the shipping agents, The Caledonian Steam Packet Company Ltd, conveys the flavour of the on-going discussions. The Minute reads as follows:

"Mr Alexander Stewart, General Manager of the shipping company, stated that the existing facilities at Larne did not justify it being classified as a passenger Port, and considered that some amenity should be provided. He was optimistic regarding the coming build-up in traffic and was of the opinion that a Terminal Building would attract more traffic.

"He said that the provision of a Terminal Building should not be treated in isolation but as part and parcel of the general amenities of the Port. Mr Stewart said that the Harbour Company should feel that the amenity must be provided and that the Port Users would be expected to contribute their quota towards its provision and upkeep."[1]

Two Larne Directors, Mr HT Browne and Mr YJ Kirkpatrick underlined that the Harbour Company had already made "a generous offer" of £12,000, which was 40 per cent of the cost of the building, but that the Government wanted them to pay 50 per cent., (plus other costs). They believed that this was unreasonable. The Larne Board also asked the shipping company to increase their annual payment on Ships' Dues from £17,000 to £21, 000. Mr Stewart undertook to talk to his Board, and it was suggested that Major MacKean , on behalf of the Larne Board, should talk to the Chairman of the Northern Ireland Tourist Board to find out if the Government's offer could be improved upon.

Construction of The Mail Quay Terminal, opened officially by the Rt. Hon Brian Faulkner, Minister of Commerce, on 7th November, 1967. In the background are vehicles waiting to embark. The Olderfleet Hotel, and the present offices of Larne Harbour Ltd., are at the top of the picture. Top right is part of the old railway station.

Some six months later, at another meeting, it was revealed that the Harbour Company's capital expenditure on the Terminal would rise to £13,500, but Mr Stewart estimated that the Company's income from the Building in terms of rent and other sources would be around £4,000 per annum. He believed that this would be a "fair return" on their capital outlay. Mr Stewart also struck an optimistic note, and said that he "anticipated that 100,000 cars per annum would be carried by the Steamers as the attraction of the Larne/Stranraer route was very bright, on account of the new roads which were being constructed in Northern Ireland."[2]

Some teething problems remained, but these were duly overcome and the Mail Quay Terminal Building was completed. It was formally opened, and appropriately so, by The Right Hon Brian Faulkner, the then Minister of Commerce, on 7 November 1967. In the relatively peaceful atmosphere of Northern Ireland in the mid-Sixties, his Ministry had been most successful in the creation of jobs and inward investment. The new Mail Quay Terminal Building became an important centre-piece in an expanding Port, and during these years the Board was continually conscious of the need to reclaim land, to improve facilities for commercial and passenger traffic, to provide sites for new businesses establishing

Another view of the construction of the Mail Quay Terminal, with large stocks of coal in the background. For many years the coal business was a mainstay of Larne Harbour. However from the mid-Fifties, coal was transferred from the quays to provide greater and cleaner facilities for container and trailer traffic. Also in the background are the remains of the old Railway Station.

Photos: opposite page & left, Browne Industrial Photographers, Larne

themselves at the Harbour, and generally to create the infrastructure for the development of a busy, modern Port.

Above: An artist's impression of the new Mail Quay Terminal, with the Caledonian Princess in the background.

On 19 July 1961, an Extraordinary General Meeting of shareholders was held at the Harbour Office, and the Directors were empowered to borrow "from time to time on behalf of the Company" an aggregate sum of up to £300,000 "for the development of the Harbour."[3] Three months earlier, the Company had bought all the former buildings of the defunct British Aluminium Company Ltd on the north-east side of the Harbour Road, plus roughly two acres of land, for £12,000.[4]

In October 1963, Mr David Logan told British Portland Cement, owners of the Magheramorne cement works, that the Harbour Company would be interested in buying the Bauxite Residue Ponds and adjoining lands to the west of Coastguard Road, covering an area of some 70 acres and known as the "Sloblands". The discussions dragged on, but in 1966 Larne Harbour Ltd bought the Sloblands (now known as the Redlands because of the residual chemical colourings) for £6,000.[5] The steady reclamation of this area is still on-going, with the use of countless tons of filling material, and it has formed the basis for much expansion at the Harbour.

Alongside Redlands, independent reclamation formed the base for the infrastructure necessary to develop a new dual carriageway to the Port, by-passing the town of Larne, to cater for the vastly increased amount of traffic travelling to and from the Harbour. During the same period there was constant up-grading of existing facilities, including the improvement of quays and ramps.

A general view of the Port of Larne in the Mid-Fifties, from the chimney of the British Aluminium Co. Limited. At one time this chimney was thought to be the biggest in Ireland. In the middle of the Lough is a Swedish vessel which off-loaded wood pulp for the Larne and Ballyclare paper mills. Some of the baled cargo can be seen in the wagons. The Mail Steamer alongside the dock is the Princess Margaret, with the smaller coaster, the Loch Etive, owned by the British Aluminium Company to the left. Directly in line with the departing vessel is the old "North Basin" area used by the Islandmagee Ferry. In the lower left-hand corner is the Pye Radio Factory, and in the lower right-hand corner are pens for cattle prior to their transportation out of Larne. Coal is stored under the crane at the bow of the Mail Steamer. Coal was usually discharged from vessels at the Middle Berth and stored adjacent to the quays.

A significant development in earlier years was the re-siting of the coal quays. For a long period of its history, Larne had been a major coal importer, and many of the Directors of Larne Harbour were or had been leading coal-importers. But as containerisation developed, the coal business declined at the port but continued to flourish elsewhere. An earlier Minute of the Board Meeting of 20 March 1957, indicated the changes; "Mr Browne agreed to consider with Mr Logan the possibility of having the Coal Traffic of Messrs Hall and MacNeice transferred from the Olderfleet Quay in order to provide greater facilities there for Container and Trailer Traffic."[6] It was clear that coal dust and clean cars and other vehicles on the new ferries did not mix!

Although Larne Harbour was gearing itself to meet the demands of developing a modern port, as well as the challenges of new labour relations in a changing industrial landscape, the composition of the Board itself and of the office staff showed relatively few changes. This was the interim period which bridged from the Post-War decades to the increasing pace, industrialisation and competitiveness of the Seventies and beyond. There was still time for practices which might seem quaint by today's standards – such as Directors having their cars washed by staff every Saturday morning while they gathered for a convivial chat and refreshments – but the office routine was strict. Although the atmosphere was friendly, everyone was expected to know his or her place.

Mrs Edna Craig, currently the Office Manager at Larne Harbour, joined the office staff on 1 February 1960, when she was only 17 years of age. She had worked previously in the book-keeping department of a local firm, but in the harbour job did not have to work all day on Saturdays. Like many other Larne people, the Harbour was part of her family history, and her husband's grandfather Andrew McIlrath worked there for 40 years, latterly as foreman fitter. Edna herself has spent almost 40 years at Larne Harbour, during which time she has seen enormous changes and improvements.

"In my early days, we worked in offices on the Harbour Road. It was a very old building, with dark tongue and groove woodwork, old mesh-framed windows, and a big coal fire in the main office. The head office girl and the juniors sat together at a large table, near a small switchboard, and the junior's job was to answer the phone. There were no individual desks as such. We sat on high three-legged stools, and we wrote with nib pens dipped in ink. However, there were no ball-point pens, and special emphasis was placed on good, clear handwriting."

These pictures show the demolition of the former property of the defunct British Aluminium Co. Ltd. in the late Fifties to make way for development at the harbour estate. The picture of the construction of new warehouses was taken on 24th May, 1961.

Discipline was strict. "We were not allowed to talk or to make phone calls, and we were definitely not allowed chewing-gum! The Company Secretary was Mr Nat Magee, and we had to go through his office to get to the toilet. If he had someone with him in the office, we had to go round the long way." Incidentally, it appears that Mr Magee may have been the "unnamed office-boy" who had been employed "on trial" in October 1914! Mr Magee, who had prospered to become Company Secretary in 1947, retired on 31 December 1973, having worked for the Company for 59 years and two months – a remarkable record of service which dates back almost exactly to October, 1914.

Edna originally looked after harbour statistics. "It was a painstaking job, demanding great accuracy. I had to record for Government use the details of everything that came into the port, and I mean everything, and I had to make monthly, quarterly and yearly returns. A great deal of the work was purely manual, but the advent of new machines made life a little easier."

An aerial view of the port in 1966 shortly after Larne Harbour Ltd. bought 70 acres from the old British Aluminium Company for £6000. The picture shows, in the background, the bauxite residue ponds, then known as "The Sloblands", now known as Redlands Estate because of the residual red chemical colourings – apparent from the photograph. The Redlands area formed the basis for much expansion at the port. Alongside Redlands, independent reclamation formed the base for the new dual carriageway. The congested quayside, in the foreground, indicates the urgent need for additional marshalling and parking space. At the quayside, left, is one of the new type of ferries on the Larne – Preston route. On the right, at Olderfleet Quay, is a small Dutch Container Vessel.

Despite what might appear today to have been somewhat Dickensian conditions, it was a happy enough office. Edna recalls "We used to let our hair down when the bosses left the office for outside meetings or for lunch, and I'm sure that they were well aware of this. The money was not great, but we had a sense of camaraderie, and I remember walking home singing from the office many a time with the others on dark nights We were probably singing to keep up our spirits in the dark, but I think we enjoyed it anyway. There were some great parties at Christmas, and every year we got a Christmas bonus of £20, which went a very long way in those days."

Like the other office staff, she was a little in awe of the Directors who, while courteous, seemed to a young girl to be very imposing figures indeed. "At Board meetings they liked to have their tea served punctually, and if it was not on time they told you off. On one occasion we pointed out that the electric kettle was on its last legs and asked for money to buy a new one. They told us to time the old kettle before buying a new model!"

Each Director had his own style. "Mr James McClenaghan, the Chairman, wore a hearing-aid, and communication with him could be difficult. He didn't like to be shouted at! Major MacKean, who succeeded him, was particularly impressive, and you felt that you really had arrived when he called you by your first name."

Edna, like many other people, was particularly fond of David Logan, who died in 1965 as General Manager and a member of the Board. During his 26 years with the Company he made an enormous contribution to the development of Larne Harbour, and won the affection and respect of everyone. His friendly, low-key manner disguised a keen brain and a good nose for business. People who knew him well recall with affection that he did much of his real business on behalf of the Harbour over a few drinks in the old King's Arms Hotel. He was popular with journalists, and one of his famous rejoinders was "When you come to see us at the Harbour, do drop in!"

Edna Craig, Office Manager at Larne Harbour Ltd., where she has worked for over 40 years. In the early days, a great deal of work was manual, but the advent of computers made life a little easier.

Photo: Alf McCreary

Edna Craig remembers him with affection and respect. "He was small, stout and paternalistic. He used to refer to us as 'his little girls'. When we asked him for an increase in salary, he would put on a mock expression of surprise and say to us 'What's wrong, has the price of shoe leather gone up?'

"Every night he would take a walk round the Harbour, with his wee dog Wendy, and that was his way of keeping in touch. He knew every member of staff, and if there was illness in any family he would bring them a present of a pot of jam from his wife. He had a great way with people. Mr Logan was never cross but he could tick you off in a manner that did not seem to be a ticking off. He was such a likeable wee man. I have vivid memories of him coming into the main office at tea-breaks and asking us, almost apologetically, if he could have a biscuit for his dog Wendy. She was just like him, low-set, roly-poly and loveable."

Miss Isabelle Logan, his daughter, is a retired school-teacher, and she still lives in Larne. A bright, vivacious woman, she has warm memories of a happy childhood when the family lived at the very heart of the Harbour, and for seven years in the house which is now the offices of Larne Harbour Ltd. She says "We were right down at the front, and I remember the sea just opposite the Olderfleet Hotel before that part had been filled in. The local anglers were plentiful then, and I recall men called Kennedy and Kell fishing for clams, in a boat called Southern Sun. I also loved going fishing with my brothers, and we used to go out in the early morning on a calm sea and bring back "dabs", a kind of flat-fish which was similar to plaice. There was always a great bustle about the Harbour, with all sorts of people coming and going. It was a wonderful place in which to grow up."

The Chairman of Larne Harbour Ltd., James McClenaghan (seated) discussing plans with senior colleagues. From left: H T Browne, a Director representing coal family interests who wrote under the pen-name "John o' the North"; a youthful Roy Esler, who was later to become Manager and Engineer; Major George MacKean, a Director and later Chairman from 1966 to 1983, who succeeded James McClenaghan on his death in 1966; and extreme right, David Logan, Harbour Manager – a respected and much-loved figure at the Port. This picture dates from May, 1959.

Her parents, obviously, were very involved with the Harbour. "My father thought the world of it, and he identified so closely with everything. I remember the awful air of desolation after the loss of the Princess Victoria. My father was absolutely devastated. He knew so many of the people involved, including Captain Ferguson, an absolute gentleman."

There were happy memories too, including a visit by the famous BBC broadcaster Richard Dimbleby who came to Larne to record the popular network radio programme "Down Your Way". "My father was interviewed and when Richard Dimbleby asked him for his choice of record, he chose the well-known song 'If I can help somebody as I pass along, then my living will not be in vain.' You have no idea how many begging letters he received after that! I also remember one of his favourite philosophies which he often quoted 'It's not the gales but the set of the sails that determines the way she goes!'

After David Logan died, the family moved house but their new home on a hill high above Larne still gives Isabelle a panoramic view of the whole Harbour area. She says "I still keep an eye on it, and I have always kept in touch with the latest developments. The Harbour, with all the memories of Daddy and Mummy and our family, is still close to my heart. That's where I spent some of the happiest days of my life, and it is still very much a part of me. I know that the same sentiments are shared by my brother Samuel, who now lives in Yorkshire."

David Logan was succeeded by Roy Esler, as Manager and Engineer of Larne Harbour Ltd. A graduate of Queen's University, Belfast in civil engineering in 1948, he joined the well-known contractors McLaughlin and Harvey Ltd of Belfast, shortly after leaving University. He was soon involved in the design and construction of new quays and hinterland at the expanding harbour. He joined the Harbour Company in 1954 as Assistant Manager and Engineer, and was involved in the further expansion of harbour facilities, along with its maintenance and the management of the stevedoring services over the next four decades, until his retirement as Director and General Manager.

David Logan was also noted for his impish sense of fun. Here he is pictured deputising for the chef and carrying in the haggis at a Larne Rotary Club luncheon. The piper was Alex Craig of Stranraer, an ex-corporal of the Highland Light Infantry.

Picture courtesy of the Belfast Telegraph

He recalls "I was fortunate in working for a private company with local Directors until 1973, during a period of unprecedented growth. During my early years with the Company, about three-quarters of my time was concentrated in engineering developments to provide quays, ramps, cranes and parking areas for the revolutionary developments in Roll-On/Roll-Off and Lift-on/Lift-off shipping which had taken place at Larne since 1948.

"The first of these services was the Atlantic Steam Navigation service which used ex-tank landing craft between Larne and Preston. I believe that Colonel Frank Bustard of ASN originally wanted to operate from Belfast but the Harbour Commission did not seem to be too interested. He then went from Belfast to Larne where David Logan welcomed him with open arms because Larne's trade had fallen seriously after the closure of the British Aluminium Company's main plant. Colonel Bustard was most impressed by David Logan and by the ramp-berth which the Port had to offer at what was known, at that time, as the War Department Quay. If it had not been for that chance contact, I suppose that Larne Harbour would not be quite what it is today."

Isabelle Logan carrying a "trophy" brought home by her father David Logan. He bought the stuffed crocodile from a hard-up sailor visiting Larne.

Photo: Alf McCreary

Roy Esler, who retired in 1987 as Manager and Engineer of Larne Harbour Ltd. "I had been at Larne Harbour in various capacities since 1948 and had seen many improvements, along with a great expansion in traffic through the Port."

Denis Galway, Director and General Manager of Larne Harbour Ltd. A Civil Engineer by profession, he "wanted to feel the fresh air round my ears and to become involved in as wide a range of activities as possible."

Roy Esler retired on 31 December 1987, shortly before his 61st birthday. He says "I had been at Larne Harbour in various capacities since 1948, and had seen many improvements, along with a great expansion in traffic through the Port. Despite a few labour problems there was always great co-operation between the management and the staff at all levels. It took both sides to make a success of the place, and I think that we succeeded in doing that."

Another noteworthy appointment during this period was that of Denis Galway on 1 January 1966, as Assistant Manager/Engineer to Roy Esler. The careers of both men were closely associated. Like Esler, Galway was a Queen's graduate in civil engineering, and his first job at the Harbour was with McLaughlin and Harvey Ltd. When Esler retired in 1987, he was succeeded as Manager by Galway, currently Director and Manager of Larne Harbour Ltd.

He remembers his first day working with McLaughlin and Harvey Ltd at the Harbour. "The Circuit of Ireland Rally ended at Larne the previous night, and it was a very late finish for me personally! I went home, changed my shirt and started work. I was only 23 at the time." Over the next few years he gained valuable experience of the major engineering developments at the Harbour, the first being the re-design and building of the coal berth at Middle Quay, while the existing quay remained operative.

He says "It was quite a feat, and I was still a relatively 'green' young engineer. The works foreman was Jimmy Davison of McLaughlin and Harvey and he was very talented, with a good brain as well as practical hands. He taught me a lot. Nowadays a man like him would have gone on straight to university. I would also like to pay tribute to the quality of all the foremen employed at the Port, down the years."

"When I was appointed in 1966 as Roy Esler's assistant, it was one of those situations where I happened to be in the right place at the right time. I did not want to follow a career at an office drawing-board. I wanted to feel the fresh air round my ears and to become involved in as wide a range of activities as possible. I always had a hankering after hydraulic and ground engineering, and also management."

He learned a great deal in a short time. "Shortly after I started with the Harbour Company, Roy Esler was off for two months with bronchitis, and I had to take over from him. I had to sink or swim, and fortunately it went reasonably well for me. I had no seafaring background, so I had to learn as I went along. I am sure that some people pulled a 'fast one' on me now and again, but if they did, they were not obvious and it had no noticeable effect."

He met many characters, not least among the dockers. "There was Rodger Johnston, the foreman, and Billy Hart, a former Sergeant-Major with a parade-ground manner, though he was a bit before my time. In those days we were more dependent on the weather for shipping movements, and that meant that we had to round up dockers at all sorts of times to unload ships. Larne was a small community, and the foremen knew where every docker would be – at home, or in the club or maybe up at his pigeon loft. I recall the well-known television reporter Fyffe Robertson making a film, and it included a shot of Rodger Johnston "knocking up" one of the dockers to help unload a ship."

"The employees' annual Harbour Trip was something else. Each year the Company subsidised an excursion for the men which, I am advised, started for some as early as 7 am, and then proceeded by bus to some hostelry which opened, in those days, at 10 am. They then moved on to places such as Londonderry, Warrenpoint or Dundalk. This was a test of endurance and stamina. But I learned a lot! The excursions took place before the days when most employees had cars."

In 1966 the death occurred of Mr James McClenaghan, the Board Chairman. He had been a Director since 1944, and Chairman for 17 years, during which time he successfully guided the Board through a most challenging period of development. He was succeeded by Major George MacKean who quickly made his own distinctive mark on the Port of Larne, and in so doing continued in the footsteps of his father Charles MacKean, thereby carrying on a long family tradition.

By the early Seventies, however, it was clear that the demands of running a modern port like Larne were stretching beyond the cost expectations of a relatively small Limited Company. Not only were there the physical developments to worry about, complex labour legislation was on the way, and it was a time when productivity agreements, work-study surveys, strategic plans and other tools of modern management were overtaking a more paternal and traditional style of operation. In March 1972 the Company increased its capital by £136,500. The Issued Capital was thus more in line with the actual capital invested in the Company, and the issue of Bonus Shares would enable the families involved to transfer shares to sons, daughters and other family members at little cost.

Darwin H Templeton, a current member of the Board, first became involved with the Port as a young accountant in the late Forties, and was appointed to the Board in 1968. He has an overview of all the major financial and other developments since that time.

"I remember going to my first Board meeting to present the accounts, and I was so overawed that I went home first and changed into my best suit! However, I found that they were friendly, and they treated me well. I eventually became a member of the Board, and I was always glad to attend, because I have a great affection for the place. They always had a lunch in the King's Arms Hotel on the day of a Board meeting. It was a ritual, and almost like a

Darwin H Templeton – "I became involved with the Port of Larne in the late Forties as a young accountant, and I have a great affection for the place."

gathering of friends rather than a Board meeting. In well over 50 years I cannot remember any rancour or ill-feeling."

Darwin Templeton also remembers Colonel Frank Bustard. "He was a gentleman, and a very shrewd businessman. He had the foresight to see the potential of a new system of moving goods by bulk. There is no doubt that this was the saviour of Larne Harbour. David Logan was another character who did a great job of running the Harbour on a shoe-string. James McClenaghan was a very good Chairman, and also a shrewd businessman. HT Browne, another Director who represented the coal family interests, was something of a literary figure who wrote for the newspaper under the pen name of "John O' The North". And latterly Major MacKean was also a most able Chairman, and a military man with a good business brain."

In July, 1973 Transport Ferry Services made history by opening up the new route between Larne and Cairnryan, but within only a few months, the Company was sold by the Bustard family to European Ferries, which owned Townsend-Thoresen. The Board of Larne Harbour Ltd was faced with the fundamental decision of finding further large sums of money to move into the modern age, or to consider selling out to European Ferries, who had expressed an interest. Darwin Templeton was one of those involved in the negotiations, together with Major MacKean. He says "The families had decided that they did not want to put up a lot of money, because many of the Directors were at an age when a large investment would have taken years to pay off and they knew that time was not on their side. So we did our homework in working out what sums we were likely to get, and we were prepared to sell, provided we got the right price. We knew that European Ferries wanted to pay a price which would keep them within the rules of the Stock Exchange, so by the time we were involved in the negotiations in London, we had a fair idea as to what we would get. They finally put forward a figure, and we left the room for a few minutes to consider their offer. We felt that we could do a bit better, and we came back and asked for more. They agreed. Our hunch had paid off! The final figure was well over £1 million, which was a good price in the circumstances, and the deal was done."

A new chapter was about to begin in the history of the Port of Larne.

1.   Minutes of the Board of the Larne Harbour Ltd, p.308.
2.   Ibid, p.322.
3.   Ibid, p.227.
4.   Ibid, p.222.
5.   Ibid, p.323.
6.   Ibid, p.152.

Spreading the message at a local Trade Fair in 1955.

THE SHAPE OF
THINGS TO COME

This April 1971 aerial photograph shows the traces of a by-gone age. Top left are the old offices of Larne Harbour Ltd., as well as old premises of the shipping and coal companies. Coal was still being stored on the quayside, though this was shortly to cease. The old rail station, so familiar in earlier photographs, has been replaced by the new terminal building. The MV Stena Nordica is approaching the quay after its journey from Stranraer. In the foreground, reclamation of the Olderfleet Bay is virtually complete. Many of the dwellings at the bottom left were later demolished to make way for the new dual carriageway. In the centre reclaimed land is already being used for parking and marshalling vehicles. This picture also illustrates the range of vessels using the Port, including Container Ships at the Continental, Olderfleet, Phoenix and Castle Quays, as well as the Preston Ferry at the Curran Quay

Photo: Agrofilms, London

157

The launch of the Caledonian Princess on
5 April 1961.

Photo: W. Ralston, Glasgow

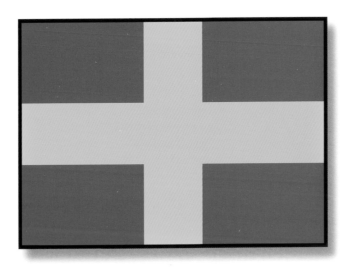

CHAPTER 11

GATEWAY TO EUROPE

The take-over by the European Ferries Group intensified the modernisation at the Port of Larne, and the expansion of facilities continued apace. New quays were developed and a Passenger Terminal was built. The passenger and freight service between Larne and Cairnryan grew in popularity. A similar service between Larne and Stranraer also developed significantly. European Ferries, which now owned the Harbour as well as operating the Larne-Cairnryan services, brought more modern business systems into operation, and there was steady growth at the Port throughout the next 15 years to 1987, when it was taken over by P&O.

The advent of European Ferries was at a time of change in the Larne-Preston service. Shareholders had been told at the AGM on 27 June 1972, that the Port had suffered a severe reduction in traffic due to the transfer of services to Belfast, which had become the preferred destination of an important customer, Containerway and Roadferry Ltd. However the Chairman, Major George MacKean, said that the Larne-Stranraer service had shown a marked increase, particularly in commercial traffic, and that further expansion was anticipated.

On 13 March 1973, the Board was informed that Mr Michael Bustard, the general Manager of the Atlantic Steam Navigation Company had intimated that the Transport Ferry Service would discontinue its thrice-weekly Preston-Larne service from 25 March because of the shortage of east-bound traffic, and because the Company was losing approximately £1,000 a day. The Board decided that of the 20 men affected by the loss of the service, four would be offered other jobs, and unfortunately that 16 would be declared redundant.

The link with Preston, which had proved so important earlier, was no longer viable. It was a tidal port, with considerable navigational difficulties, and this proved to be a drawback in keeping the business of hauliers who wanted a regular service which did not depend on the changes in the tides. Another major turn-off was a prolonged dock dispute at Preston in 1969 which undermined its reputation for good labour relations, and the Port lost favour. It simply could not compete in a highly-competitive market, and went into decline.

The purchase of Larne Harbour Ltd by the European Ferries Group was formally agreed by the shareholders and the Board at special meetings early in October 1973, and the new arrangements were given an added bonus shortly afterwards by the settlement of a long-standing inter-union dispute. On 21 November, the Chairman Major MacKean informed the Board that the General and Municipal Workers Union and the Amalgamated Transport and General Workers' Union had finally agreed to negotiate with the Company on a joint basis.

The origin of the dispute lay in the contravention of the Company's agreement with the GMWU whereby only its members could be employed at the Port. On 23 October 1970, 59 employees had to be dismissed because of their decision to discontinue membership of the GMWU and to affiliate with the AGTWU.

The dispute was eventually referred by the Minister of Health and Social Services to a Court of Inquiry, under the Chairmanship of Professor JC Wood. The Report noted that "as an agreement between the Unions had not been reached, Mr Victor Feather, General Secretary of the Transport and General Workers' Union intervened in the dispute and on 29 October 1971, reported to the Secretary of the Court of Inquiry that the two Unions had agreed to a solution to the difficulty. In effect, the Court of Inquiry adheres to the recommendation of Mr Feather that the two Unions have joint representation at Larne Harbour."[2] However, the local representative of the GMWU was averse to joint representation, and the Board agreed to take no action "pending further developments." It took another two years for all sides to agree on joint representation.

Announcement of the new passenger ferry service from Larne to Cairnryan 10 July, 1973.

Roy Esler, the then Manager and Engineer recalls "The ATGWU official was Sam McVeigh who had been a docker in Belfast and had the reputation of being a fierce man, but when I retired he sent me a personal note saying how much he had been surprised by our treatment of him at his first attendance at the Joint Consultative Committee when he had expected us to give him a rough time, but I think he soon realised we were good employers!"

The Port of Larne, like all other harbours, reflected the developments concerning labour over the years. In 1947 the casualisation of dock labour in Great Britain took place, only to be decasualised in 1969. There was a national seamen's strike in 1966, minor local labour trouble in June, 1970, and a National Strike of Dock Workers in July of that year.

In 1971 the Company made two employees redundant because of "the installation of a new Hydraulic Vehicle Ramp at the Continental Quay which will necessitate the appointment of a competent operator."[3] They had worked previously on a manually-operated ramp. Their Union, the TGWU fought their case, and it was referred by the then Minister of Health and Social Services, Mr William K Fitzsimmons, to economist Dr William Black of Queen's University, Belfast. He concluded that "the introduction of the new ramp does not justify the redundancy of one man." The Board asked its Chairman to inform the Minister of Health and Social services that the Directors accordingly accepted the findings of the inquiry.[4]

In the Seventies, Larne Harbour as a major port was caught up in two politically-motivated disputes, the first of which brought Northern Ireland virtually to a standstill. This was the Loyalist Ulster Workers Council Strike from 15-28 May 1974, which led to the downfall of the Northern Ireland Executive, the first experiment in truly cross-community Government. It was ironic that this so-called "Power-sharing Executive" was brought down by a well-planned series of stoppages by electricity power-workers, and also by road-blocks, intimidation and threats by the Loyalist rank and file. The cutting of power supplies and the extensive Loyalist paramilitary activity caused chaos, and after 14 days the Unionist members resigned from the Executive, thus rendering it ineffective.[5]

Dougie Hood

Dougie Hood, for 37 years the boatman on the Islandmagee ferry, just like his father and grandfather before him. 'I enjoyed every minute.' Now retired, one of his hobbies is making models of ships.

Photo: Alf McCreary

One of the institutions of the Port of Larne is the Islandmagee Ferry which makes the short crossing at regular intervals daily and saves travellers a 20 mile detour by road from the harbour. According to ancient legend, St Patrick himself made the crossing in a coracle and, as a result, the ferryman and his successors were given Divine immunity from accident or danger!

Dougie Hood, now in his early Eighties, worked on the Islandmagee Ferry for a lifetime, as did his father and grandfather who were the proprietors before him. Initially Dougie worked in the Belfast shipyard for 16 years but spent the next 37 as the boatman ferrying countless passengers across the narrow channel of Larne Lough in all weathers.For many years his assistant was Sammy McCalmont, a man of slow words and of even slower speeds across the water.

Dougie recalls "We took everyone over, workers to the Ballylumford Power station, people who wanted to shop in Larne, football supporters, farmers, young people going to the Laharna Ballroom (and waiting for them on the way back when they lingered among the container wagons with their partners from the dance) and even people going to church! Some of the young Larne men kept a bachelors' abode in Islandmagee and they would go across to church on a Sunday. On the way back some of them would sit in the boat and sing hymns, and then they would march back up the road till you heard the singing in the distance."

A typical view of the Islandmagee ferry as it crosses Larne Lough.

"We also carried livestock, and that could be tricky. The cows swam across and you held them by a halter, but they were hard to get into the water. The farmers also took sheep, and once you got the first one on board the others followed. It was the same at the far end, but what a mess!"

"It was a hard job, but it was healthy. I was never frightened, but I always respected the sea. Sometimes you had to be very careful when a nor'west was blowing and you had to judge how the sea would hit you. On the day of the Princess Victoria disaster my father, who used to take lighthousemen to and from the Maidens, was shipwrecked in his boat. The engine stopped and he was carried onto the rocks near the light-house. My daughter was with him, and he was able to fling her into the arms of the light-house keeper. That night we heard about the Princess Victoria, and it was very, very sad. We knew many of the people on that boat.

"There were good times on the Islandmagee Ferry. You met a lot of people, and you would share things with them. Many a time I would share my cigarettes on the way across and they would share theirs with me on the way back. It was great 'crack'. I enjoyed every minute, and I miss it now. People had a smile on their faces, in those times. They were happy days."

Dougie Hood (right) in his hey-day, with his assistant, the late Sammy McCalmont – a man of slow words and even slower speeds across the Lough.

A picture of the ferry, dwarfed by a cross-channel vessel.

Photo: Alf McCreary

There were four power stations in Northern Ireland – one at Coolkeeragh in Co. Londonderry, two in Belfast, and the fourth at Ballylumford, just across the Lough on the Islandmagee side of Larne Harbour. "The nightmare that permanently clouded the vision of the Executive and of the British Ministers was of a province totally without power; of a community in which every mechanical device from the telephone to the electric light, from the petrol pump to the hospital iron lung, from the incubator to the water supply and sewerage system ceased to function."[6]

Given such high political stakes in the battle between the Government and the Loyalists, it was inevitable that the Port of Larne would be a target for disruption. The author and journalist Robert Fisk noted the upheaval caused on the first day of the strike. "At Larne, where the ferries leave daily for the Scottish port of Stranraer, masked UDA men in camouflage jackets and carrying heavy wooden clubs roamed the streets around the docks. Wearing UDA insignia, they called methodically at every shop in the town and ordered their owners to close down. Several uniformed men hijacked cars and lorries and placed them across the harbour roads, cutting off two engineering works and preventing the sailing of the Irish Sea Ferry."[7] During the strike a number of ferries were able to operate, but mainly carrying vehicles with drivers. These could be despatched relatively easily provided the Harbour authorities were able to have the loading and unloading ramps properly manned. A number of employees courageously defied intimidation and turned up for work as best they could.

By 27 May the power stations began their final run down and an electricity spokesman spoke ominously of the Province reaching "the point of no return". The next day Brian Faulkner, the Unionist leader and his colleagues resigned, and the Executive collapsed. The power-sharing experiment had failed ignominiously, and it was virtually a quarter of a century before another similar body was tentatively contemplated. The dark symmetry of history had embraced Larne Harbour twice, in extremely serious Loyalist threats to the rule of law and to the authority of the British Government - once during the gun-running crisis of 1914, and then in the UWC strike in 1974.

There was further serious disruption in May 1977 during a politically-motivated strike backed by the United Unionist Action Council. However the then Secretary of State Roy Mason took a more robust approach in dealing with insurrection than his predecessors had done, the strike had less political backing and, even more significantly, the Loyalists failed to halt electricity supplies. However there were considerable disruptions at Larne again, and a number of Larne Harbour employees showed courage and independence of mind in doing what they could to keep the ferries in operation. On 18 May, 1977 the Board of Larne Harbour Ltd noted that the strike had "interrupted shipping" and expressed its appreciation of "the efforts made by Management, Staff, Harbour Police and some workmen to restore services during this difficult period."

These politically-motivated strikes were exceptional, and the labour relations at the Port were generally good. One man who saw many changes is Jim Agnew. He started work in Larne as a docker in 1952, and carried out several roles as a coal filler, then a crane-driver, and eventually retired in December, 1991 as foreman stevedore. He estimates that, during this time, the numbers of dockers and associated workers decreased from 80 to over 50. From the early Seventies, with gradual reduction in LO/LO operations there were changes in working practices on board ships. The crews, rather than stevedores, increasingly did the lashing for vehicles, and there was less bulk and general cargo work.

He recalls "There were big changes in my time. During my early days there was a lot of manual labour, and there were all kinds of vessels using the port. There were timber boats, pulp boats for the local paper mills, boats with iron ore, coal boats, vessels with animal foodstuffs, and even boats carrying ammunition. It was all hard work, and on many a cold morning with the wind whistling round your ears, you were glad to get into the shelter of the ship's hold.

"There was also a great technique in the work. You picked up many tips from older colleagues. For

Jim Agnew, who started as a docker in 1952 and retired as foreman stevedore in December 1991. 'There were big changes in my time.'

example when handling bales of pulp, which were cumbersome and heavy, you did not so much lift them as manoeuvre them into place. As time went on you learned different techniques, and there was less manual work. There was better equipment and you had better working conditions. I must say that I enjoyed my time at the Harbour, and I had some great colleagues. Larne Harbour was good to me, and I hope that I was also good to it!"

Another man with a long history of working at Larne is Robert Hoy, who retired in March 1987 as a ramp operator after 46 years service. He started work in 1941 as a labourer at the age of 20. His father, also called Robert, worked at the Harbour as a waterman and a fire-lighter, but Robert junior did not ask his father's help to get him a job. He asked the best man possible – David Logan, the Harbour Manager, who told him to start work on the next Monday at 8 am.

He recalls "I have vivid memories of the war years. I remember the troops passing through here for training in Northern Ireland and then coming back through again on their way to the Normandy landings. After the war, things were a bit grim for a while. There was still rationing, and you had to learn to do without. I don't think that anyone went hungry as such. Even with rationing, there was enough to go around."

"Life got back to normal slowly. After a time as a labourer I was trained to be a crane driver, and I remember the days when we had to lift vehicles on board the Mail Steamer for Stranraer. Then we moved to the container traffic on the top deck, but I remember that there were only two or three at first. Later I was trained to be a ramp operator and I worked with

vessels like the Empire Doric. It was hard work, but those were happy days."

He was awarded the BEM in the 1976 New Year's Honours List. He says "It was a wonderful reward for my work. I remember the Investiture very well. My wife and my son Robert were with me. I have some very happy memories of my time at Larne Harbour". Incidentally the Board at Larne, during their meeting on 21 January 1976 noted the award to Mr Hoy and offered their congratulations. It was a good example of a Company that, despite the business challenges of the times, was still thoughtful enough to retain the human touch.

From the late Sixties and early Seventies, the harbour facilities were greatly enhanced, with vast improvements to marshalling areas, the demolition of old buildings, the provision of new ramps, and the modernisation of quays. In the mid-Sixties there had been numerous small offices and buildings,

Bobby Hoy BEM, who retired as a crane driver and ramp operator in 1987 after 46 years service. 'It was hard work but those were happy days.'

Photo: Alf McCreary

including a Post Office, and a Launch House where all slings and ropes were spliced, and thimbles inserted. The old Harbour Office had a first floor which included dull and dingy offices. It was here that draughtsman Tom Whitehead, an ex-heating and ventilating engineer who retired in 1968, kept the Company's drawings up to date. The present offices – in a house called Wulfrichford (the ancient name for Larne from Viking times) – provide a marked contrast to those earlier premises, though prior to the extension in 1982, many of the staff worked in fairly confined conditions.

Some of the old Aluminium Works buildings were demolished, and others were converted for use as warehouses and workshops. The former workshops were a series of small buildings, in the Old Harbour Yard, where the Passenger Terminal is now situated. Near the transit shed for Anglo-Continental Container Services, a Monobox crane was erected in the 1960's. However this travelling gantry was blown over in a storm in 1972, and the site, leased from Larne Harbour Ltd, was surrendered in the mid-Seventies. The transit sheds for ACCS, latterly Containerway and Roadferry, were also surrendered in the early-Seventies.

The Burmah Oil Company, formerly Lobitos, had tanks at the end of Fleet Street, on the site of the present short-stay car park. These were demolished and the site was surrendered in 1980. Until the new dual carriageway was opened in 1977, all traffic from the Port went up Fleet Street, along Curran Road, and through the town of Larne, thus causing severe congestion. This was intensified as the arrival of the afternoon ferry from Stranraer tended to coincide with workers coming out of the old Pye Radio (later the STC) factory. Although the opening of the dual carriageway dramatically improved the traffic flow, there were still

bottlenecks. The first Passenger Terminal is still in existence at MacKean Quay, and was an important facility for travellers. It replaced the old Station Building but the level crossing still restricted vehicle movements when passengers were moving to or from the Stranraer boat train. Incidentally, part of the infill for the reclamation area which formed the base for the new dual carriageway was surplus rock obtained from the Magheramorne Cement Works quarry, owned by Blue Circle plc. The land for the dual carriageway ending at the Terminal roundabout was granted by Larne Harbour Ltd to the developers.

Mrs Iris Concannon, wife of Don Concannon MP, Minister of State for Northern Ireland, cuts the tape to open the Chaine Quay and two-tier ramp – the first in Ireland – on 27th June 1978. On the left is Major George B MacKean, then Chairman of Larne Harbour Ltd. In the background is Mr Concannon, to the right of his wife. On the far left is Keith Wickenden, Chairman of European Ferries, alongside local MP and Mayor of Larne, Mr Roy Beggs.

Not surprisingly, the major modernisation of the Port changed the landscape dramatically. The Chaine Quay, named after James Chaine who had put Larne on the map as a port in the 19th century was completely re-developed and formally opened on 27 June 1978. Approximately a year later, the Continental Quay, which had also been significantly re-developed, was formally opened on 17 May 1979. The two new quays provided double-deck ramps, the first in Ireland, and were installed to cater for the simultaneous working of both decks of the new vessels which were coming into operation on the Irish Sea at that time.

Previously, vehicle discharge from two-deck vessels was carried out on the lower level, using internal ship's ramps, or lifts from the upper deck. In some cases, vehicles were lifted off the upper deck by cranes. Two-deck loading had considerable advantages, particularly on multi-purpose vessels carrying cars, passengers and freight vehicles. Cars could be loaded separately from commercial vehicles, thus reducing the turnaround times.[8]

Rodger Johnston, Harbour Foreman, at the new Chaine Quay ramp in 1978.

With the large investment involved in these new facilities, it was essential to ensure that they could cater for the widest possible variety of current and future vessels. To this end, Larne utilised a "variable finger concept" which they had pioneered in 1971. In simple terms, any combination of "fingers" could be lowered, thus catering for ships of varying beams, and doors or openings of different widths. The Harbour facilities were specifically designed to provide flexibility in dealing with a wide range of vessels, rather than for a special type of vessel. Incidentally, the large multi-purpose vessels which were first introduced on the Irish sea from 1967 provided greater vehicle headroom and drive-through capability. This helped to reduce the reversing operations, with a consequent reduction in turnaround time at the port. In 1966 16ft curved-top containers were the norm, whereas RO/RO vehicles now exceed 15 metres in length.

One of the benefits to shipping was the dredging of a nine-metre channel to the jetty serving the new Ballylumford Power Station which had been completed in the late Sixties. This meant that large vessels could come into the Port more easily and swing inside the Lough, rather than having to turn outside and come in stern first, as had been the norm. The Port's coal fillers, or labourers, in addition to working on vessels at Larne, also discharged coal boats at the Power Station.

The customer was always of paramount importance, and Larne built up an envied reputation as a good Port for hauliers. Shortly after the take-over by European Ferries, however, concern was expressed by Ferrymasters, owned by P&O who had been trading to Larne for more than 20 years. The Company was concerned that Transport Ferry Service, who were owned by European Ferries, might gain unfair trading advantages.

The Larne Board, after meeting P&O representatives, stated "It is the policy of the Company to continue to operate the port as heretofore on a commercial basis, where no preferential treatment will be given to any port user in respect of Ships' Dues, Cargo Dues, Stevedoring

Charges or the allocation of berths".[9] This matter continued to exercise the minds of both parties for some considerable period, and a satisfactory agreement was reached in September 1975 with Pandoro Ltd., concerning the Larne – Fleetwood route.

The loss of the Preston link was more than offset by the development of the new Larne-Cairnryan service, which was inaugurated on 10 July 1973, by the Ionic Ferry, with Captain William Close of Larne in command. One man who remembers the day well is Park Wilson who worked at Larne for 41 years and retired as Port Manager with P&O European Ferries. He recalls "News of the Cairnryan service found its way into the Press and we had an enormous response because this was just before the start of the big holiday rush in Northern Ireland. We could have filled the vessel, but it was decided to start with only 80 passengers. We built up the service gradually, and began taking more freight. Within a comparatively short time we were able to generate business for two vessels on the route and I believe that we provided a very good service."

Commercial users appreciated the short crossing and the quick turnaround at each end. Park Wilson, who worked with a wide variety of hauliers in his time, recalls "The lorry-drivers were a breed apart. They just lived and breathed lorry-driving. All they wanted was a short crossing, a good meal, the chance of a quick nap, and out on the road again. There were many great characters, including Sam Barr who had only one eye. He could reverse a huge lorry better with one eye than many another driver with two!"

Park Wilson, who has a farm near Larne, worked for 41 years at the harbour, and retired as Port Manager with P&O European Ferries. 'All the lorry drivers wanted was a short crossing, a good meal, a quick nap, and out on the road again.'

There was also a wide range of freight customers. "They varied from one man with a lorry to some of the big companies with a fleet of vehicles. In the early days money seemed easier to come by, but as competition began to bite, the inefficient hauliers fell away. The ones who survived had thought out the business. They worked on economic rates, and organised the loads both ways, not just going across and hoping to get a load on the way back.

"There were so many different companies and cargoes that I have almost lost track of them. Those were the days when we had big industrial companies like Courtaulds, ICI and British Enkalon. We had freight of all kinds – fibres, livestock, hazardous cargoes, and large quantities of fruit. Every weekend we handled a cargo of bananas which had been driven north from Cork for transport to Scotland and the British mainland. Don't ask me why it had to be that way, but we always called it the 'Banana Boat'. It was all part of the bustle and variety of Larne in those days." A number of people, including Ted Percival and Leone Donkin, were prime movers in establishing a new link between Larne and Fleetwood.

Pandoro's Larne to Fleetwood RO/RO service began on 23 February, 1975, replacing the earlier LO/LO service operated by Ferrymasters until 20 February of the same year. Northern Ireland Trailers Ltd. had operated a similar LO/LO service to Preston until 26 February 1975, and a LO/LO service to Ardrossan from August 1956 to April 1971 and Burns and Laird operated a RO/RO service to the same Port from January 1971 to February 1976.

Though freight was the 'bread and butter' traffic for the Harbour, there were considerable developments in passenger traffic between Larne and Stranraer from the Mid-Fifties onwards. Following the tragic loss of the Princess Victoria in January 1953, the Hampton Ferry was switched from Dover to Stranraer in June of that year to help the regular ferry, the Princess Margaret, each summer, until 1961. The previous year the Larne-Stranraer route was transferred by the British Transport Commission to the Caledonian Steam Packet Company (Irish Services Ltd), and its vessels were resplendent in the bright new Caledonian insignia, including the Company's yellow flag with a red lion rampant.

In 1957 the British Transport Commission ordered a new vessel from Wm Denny and Bros of Dumbarton, and the splendid new Caledonian Princess was launched on 5 April 1961, and began her service between Larne and Stranraer in December. She was turbine-propelled and was larger than the two previous car ferries, which were fitted with diesel engines. She also had superior passenger accommodation, and could carry a total of 1,400 travellers. There were sleeping-berths for 82 first-class passengers, and 94 second-class berths. The main deck could carry over 100 cars, or their equivalent, and there was provision for motor-bikes, and even push-bikes. As one familiar and reliable observer noted "Nothing had been spared in making the new ship the show-piece of Scottish shipping, and this was reflected in the final cost of £1,840,000 – ten times the cost of Princess Margaret."[10]

With the Caledonian Princess now in service, the Princess Margaret was sold to a Hong Kong shipping company for a reported £45,000 and renamed the Macau, plying as a ferry between Hong Kong and the Portuguese colony of the same name. However in 1971 she became a victim of the infamous Typhoon Rose which hit Hong Kong and was so badly damaged that she never sailed again. In March 1974, she was handed over to the ship-breakers.[11]

In March 1963, the British Railways Board published the wide-ranging and radical Beeching Report, which recommended the closure of the railways serving Stranraer. This understandably caused consternation to the supporters of the Larne-Stranraer route, but after strong representations the Government kept open the line to Glasgow, thus maintaining the train link to the rest of Great Britain.

On 24 April 1967, the Antrim Princess was launched, and in subsequent years a series of "Princess" vessels provided the mainstay of the service between Larne and Stranraer, in the livery of British Rail, with a red funnel, and white double arrows on a blue hull. The British

Railways Board had taken over the service through British Transport Ship Management (Scotland) Ltd. In 1969 an order for a sister ship to the Antrim Princess was placed with an Italian company which – despite a predictable outcry from British shipbuilding interests – had won the contract, and the Ailsa Princess was delivered on 22 June 1971. She then made a nine-day voyage from Venice to Stranraer, taking up service on 7 July.

By the mid-Seventies "the route had been transformed since 1961 to a profitable service carrying over 200,000 vehicles and 680,000 passengers each year."[12] The Caledonian Princess had played a major part in this success. "Within two years, the profit on the ship's working was £370,000 – almost double the profit of 1961. There is no doubt that the Caledonian Princess was the ship that changed the route's fortunes . . . She was the ship that provided the foundations for an industry which is hardly recognisable compared to that for which she sowed the seeds of success back in December 1961."[13]

The closure of the Belfast-Heysham service in 1975 generated more business for the Larne routes to Cairnryan and Stranraer, and in October 1977, Sealink - now the operating company for British Rail - announced another new vessel for the Stranraer

An invitation to a short cruise on the virtually new Antrim Princess on 5 December 1967.

CALEDONIAN STEAM PACKET COMPANY LIMITED ANNAN

Mr. G. W. STEWART, C.V.O., Chairman and Managing Director, Caledonian Steam Packet Group,

requests the pleasure of the company of

MRS E. POLLOCK .... and Lady

aboard T.S.S. ANTRIM PRINCESS, the new ship for the Stranraer–Larne route, for a short cruise on Tuesday, December 5, 1967.

Luncheon

Timetable overleaf

R.S.V.P. Secretary, Caledonian Steam Packet Co. Ltd., Gourock

run. On 24 May 1979, the new Galloway Princess was launched, with the increased capacity for 1,000 passengers and 300 cars. However, her completion was delayed by around ten months, and she did not leave for her trials off Scotland until 9 March 1980. She was handed over on 22 April, and her maiden voyage was on 1 May.[14]

In December 1983, the Antrim Princess suffered a serious engine-room fire after leaving Larne, and RAF helicopters rescued around 128 passengers and 23 crew off the Antrim coast. However, the ship's Captain and 30 crew members stayed on board, and later on the vessel regained some power. After lying off Larne overnight, she was towed the next day to Belfast for repairs.[15] Despite such mishaps, and the earlier loss of the Princess Victoria, the vessels on the Larne routes had a good safety record.

In July 1984, the Government sold Sealink UK Ltd. to Sea Containers for £66 million. The Antrim Princess remained on the Scottish route until October, 1985, and from 1986 the Galloway Princess and the St David, which had deputised for the Antrim Princess after her mishap, covered the Larne-Stranraer run.[16]

By the early Eighties, the increase in passengers necessitated the construction of a new multi-user Passenger Terminal in Larne, although the Mail Quay Terminal building had provided an important facility for travellers since 1967. The design and siting of the terminal was important, and careful thought had to be given to the safety, security and comfort of passengers, and the segregation of passenger and commercial vehicles.

After much consideration, it was decided to site the Terminal adjacent to the Harbour entrance, as well as car parks and the railway station. Bus parking was provided at the back of the Terminal, and there was covered access at a high level for foot passengers between the Terminal and the vessels. Access from the elevated walkway to the ships was provided by a specially-constructed connecting gangway, which could be raised or lowered according to tidal variations and the level of each vessel's doors. In parallel, Northern Ireland Railways decided to modernise its Larne Harbour Station, linked directly to the new Terminal for the convenience of passengers. The Terminal was completed in 1985 and opened on 13 November by Dr Rhodes Boyson, Minister of State for Northern Ireland. The new Terminal also removed the need for a level crossing, which had previously caused delays to traffic in the harbour complex.

The major development of facilities at Larne was a considerable challenge to the Company, and was financed through investment by Larne Harbour Ltd., with assistance from the European Regional Development Fund, as well as Government and bank loans. As early as June 1974, the Board assumed a capital expenditure up to 1980 of £3.5 millions.[17] On 19 January 1977, the Board agreed that the major construction on the new RO/RO berth with a two-tier ramp at the Chaine/Middle quay should go ahead but only subject to a series of stringent conditions, including Government confirmation that a new passenger charge could be levied, and that the development scheme would continue to qualify for a grant from the European Regional Development Fund.[18]

Port charges were sometimes a bone of contention with the shipping operators. For example, there was a dispute between the Board and BTSM (S) concerning increased passenger charges. A Government Inquiry found in the Port's favour. Sealink (Scotland) Ltd, its successor from 3 March 1980, also became involved in a dispute with the Board about the terms of a 1939 agreement between Larne Harbour Limited and the old LMS Company. This, by agreement, went to arbitration, and in return for a payment of £30,000 compensation from Larne, Sealink (Scotland) Ltd legally surrendered the rights to the use of the Mail Quay.[19] In October 1981 the Board was informed that an agreement with Pandoro Ltd concerning its RO/RO freight services between Larne and Liverpool and Fleetwood would be renewed for a further seven years, and after negotiation, a new agreement was signed in June 1985.

Main Picture: The new walkway from the terminal to the Chaine Quay provided protection for passengers in all weathers.

Inset: Construction of the new passenger terminal at Larne, completed and opened in 1985.

Photos: Browne of Larne

During these years there were significant Board changes, due to the untimely passing of two Chairmen in relatively quick succession. On 7 May 1983, the death occurred of Major George MacKean, who had been a Director since 27 August 1947, and Chairman from 1 August 1966. The Board expressed its great sadness, and sympathy with the family, noting that the late Major MacKean's "influence and presence at Larne Harbour will be enormously missed."Shortly afterwards the Board decided that "As a memorial to the late Chairman Major MacKean, and to the MacKean family connection with the Company since 1912, the 'Mail Quay' be re-named MacKean Quay to perpetuate the family name at the Harbour."[20]

Just two months after Major MacKean's death, the Board received another blow through the death of the new Chairman Mr KD Wickenden on 9 July 1983, as the result of a crash in a light aeroplane at Shoreham, Sussex. Keith Wickenden, a Director of the parent Company European Ferries Ltd. and an MP, had only been appointed Chairman of Larne Harbour Ltd on 19 May 1983. He was succeeded as Chairman by Mr Geoffrey Parker.

Throughout the years of ownership by European Ferries Ltd, the finances of Larne Harbour remained sound, although it was caught up in large-scale financial transactions by the parent company, which borrowed considerable amounts from British and German banks. The parent company also had considerable investments overseas. Its luxurious La Manga Club in Southern Spain was in good shape, but the Group's main problems stemmed from its US investments, particularly in Houston, Texas which had been badly hit by falling oil prices. Overall the Group's profits were substantially down, and it was difficult to see how it could continue to trade on its own without continuing to make substantial losses.[21]

Despite the parent Company's difficulties, Larne Harbour Ltd continued to record healthy profits. In 1985, for example, it made a profit, after tax, of £2.3 million, compared to £1.4 million for the previous year. The profit for the year ended 31 December 1986, was £2,559,800. Despite the larger business worries of European Ferries Ltd, it seemed as if Larne Harbour Ltd would continue to trade profitably and to continue to develop the Port to the highest standards. But the New Year was to bring dramatic changes. European Ferries Ltd was taken over by P&O, and a new subsidiary Company – P&O European Ferries Ltd – was formed. The Board Minutes of 4 February 1987 contain one short but significant reference to the latest developments: "The Chairman reported that following the European Ferries Group merger in January 1987 with the Peninsular and Oriental Steam Navigation Company there will be Administrative changes."

The shape of things to come – an article from the Liverpool Daily Post, 24 December 1985, reporting the takeover of European Ferries by P&O.

This model of studied understatement underlined the significant new changes that had already taken place.

P and O clear the decks for a takeover

by William Leece

SHIPPING to construction group P and O put a boarding party on the Townsend Thoresen group European Ferries yesterday in a £36m deal.

P and O took control of nearly 21 per cent of the European Ferries' shares and its chairman Sir Jeffrey Sterling is to join the EF board.

Optimistic speculators had been hoping for an all-out takeover bid and as trading wound down before Christmas, shares in both companies slipped on the Stock Exchange.

P and O was able to but its stake in European Ferries through the back door, it was revealed yesterday. Two European Ferries directors, John Dick and William Pauls, own a company between them which in its turn has a 20.8 per cent stake in EF.

P and O's move was to buy 50.1 per cent of the Dick/ Pauls company, giving it control of the whole of its share block, at a price equivalent ot 125p a share.

Sir Jeffrey's only comment yesterday was to say that he saw the holding in European Ferries as "a strategic trade investment. European Ferries has a very down to earth management which knows its business."

However, veteran Sterling-watchers were soon predicting that a full bid would eventually follow. Sir Jeffrey's softly-softly style, they argued, meant that he was likely to build up a stake in a would-be target and establish friendly relations before trying for an agreed bid.

P and O also has a 13 per cent stake in the Liverpool-based shipping and industrial services group Ocean Transport and Trading and most observers believe a bid will eventually come despite repeated denials from Sir Jeffrey.

Yesterday's move for the European Ferries share damped down hopes that the bid would come sooner rather than later, and shares in Ocean also moved down on the Stock Exchange.

The deal with the two European Ferries directors also gives P & O a number of indirect investments.

European Ferries has a number of property interests in the United States—an area where P & O has said it wants to invest—and has a share in the property group Stockley, which in its turn has a stake in another property company, Stock Conversion.

Sir Jeffrey Sterling

Nellie the Elephant packed her trunk . . . and set off for the Townsend Thoresen ferry from Cairnryan to Larne. She was part of a circus visiting Northern Ireland.

1.   Larne Harbour Ltd Board Minutes 21 October 1970, p.397.
2.   Op.Cit. p.423.
3.   Op.Cit. p.415.
4.   Op.Cit. p.418.
5.   WD Flackes and S Elliott "Northern Ireland – A Political Directory" p.289. Published by the Blackstaff Press, Belfast.
6.   Robert Fisk "The Point of No Return" pp.168-170, published by Andre Deutsch London.
7.   Op.Cit. p.59.
8.   DP Galway in a paper to the Institution of Civil Engineers (Transportation Section) and Chartered Institute of Transport, 25 January 1988.
9.   Larne Harbour Ltd Board Minutes, 21 November 1973, p.464.
10. Op.Cit. G Fraser MacHaffie, p.170.
11. Ibid. p.172.
12. Miles Cowsill "Stranraer – Larne, The Car Ferry Era", Ferry Publications, p.26.
13. Op.Cit. John Hendy, pp.45-46.
14. Op.Cit. pp.26-27
15. Op.Cit. p.31.
16. Op.Cit. pp.33-34.
17. Larne Harbour Ltd Board Minutes, p.476.
18. Op.Cit. p.520.
19. Ibid. p.692.
20. Ibid. p.647.
21. Sunday Times Business Section, 7 December 1986.

The Russian vessel Sedov, part of the
spectacular Tall Ships Race of 1991, during a
courtesy visit to the Port of Larne.

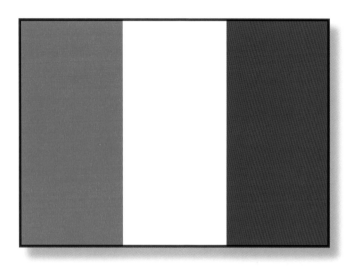

CHAPTER 12

INTO THE NEW MILLENNIUM

As the new Millennium approached, the last 13 years of the 20th century brought accelerated progress at Larne. Significant improvements were made at the Port. The Mail Quay was totally re-developed and re-named, and the Curran Quay was also re-developed. In 1996 a £2 million high-technology Distribution Centre for the storage of fresh and chilled produce was opened on the Redlands Estate, and in 1998 a new Freight Check-in Centre was built for commercial traffic. A year later, a £2.2 million extension to the Distribution Centre was undertaken, to meet increasing demand from customers.

There was more upbeat news from P&O European Ferries, who announced in June, 1999 a £4.5 million development for Cairnryan. The new facility was planned to include separate reception areas for tourist and freight traffic, new booking and information offices, a baggage-handling area and facilities for children and the disabled.

The project was part-financed by the European Regional Development Fund, secured with the assistance of Dumfries and Galloway Council. It also included landscaping and environmental improvements to upgrade the port area boundary and its interface with the local A77 road.

The continued commercial confidence at Larne was underlined by significant additions to the shipping fleet. In February 1999, P&O European Ferries announced an order for a new 21,000 ton passenger and freight ferry from Mitsubishi of Japan, to begin service in mid-summer 2000. The new vessel, with a speed of 23 knots, was designed to reduce the travelling time on the conventional ferry to Cairnryan to just 105 minutes - a reduction of 25 per cent on the time taken by the older vessels. The competitive edge to modern ferry travel from Larne had been sharpened some three years earlier with the introduction of the powerful new P&O Jetliner, a high-speed ferry with an operating speed of 32 knots, thus

An artist's impression of the new passenger terminal at Cairnryan – part of a £4.5m investment in the Scottish port.

reducing the Cairnryan crossing to only one hour, the fastest on the Irish Sea. For the further convenience of passengers, a new Call Centre was opened in 1998, and in 1999 P&O introduced a fifth vessel to the route - thus more than doubling the provision of only five years previously. Overall, the Port moved into the new Millennium on a sound commercial footing, and this was in no small measure due to its strength in depth as part of the P&O Group.

The shape of things to come. An artist's impression of the new ferry, the European Causeway, for the Larne–Cairnryan route.

When P&O launched an agreed bid for European Ferries in 1986, it did not take the City by surprise. Such a move had been expected, in the face of European Ferries' worsening financial position. Earlier, the P&O Group had taken a 20.8 per cent stake in European Ferries in a deal worth £36 millions. The P&O Chairman, Sir Jeffrey Sterling (now Lord Sterling of Plaistow) described this as "a strategic trade investment."[1] The deal was described in the February 1986 edition of Money Observer as potentially one of the shrewdest moves that Sir Jeffrey had made. "For it affords him a variety of fascinating options for expansion in both the shipping and property worlds."

On 5 December 1986, following clearance by the Monopolies Commission, P&O bid £286.8 millions for European Ferries. The London Times described this as "a rescue operation", and quoted Sir Jeffrey as saying "There is a compelling logic to this deal which should be to everyone's advantage."

The distinctive P&O Flag – with the red and gold of the Spanish Royal house of Aragon and Castile, and the blue and white of the Portuguese Braganzas – symbolises the company's origins in serving the Iberian Peninsula in the 19th century. The story of the Port of Larne later became part of the world-wide history of P&O.

The Times continued "The takeover gives P&O control of the leading cross-Channel ferry group Townsend Thoresen, and the ports of Felixstowe and Larne. In backing the deal, the Board of European Ferries concedes that on its own it would have faced severe difficulties and expects a very substantial drop in profits for the current year. The company has been hit by a 10-week stoppage on services from Felixstowe, and by the slump in the US property market.

"The Directors say that the strikes will be responsible for £10 millions of lost profits in 1986, while in the US its property profits, normally

generated towards the end of the year, will be eliminated. Last year, its property activities in Houston and Denver contributed £17 millions profit, but they are expected to be wiped out after write-offs for carrying costs in Houston.

"European Ferries made £48 millions last year, but according to market sources, it is expected to make only half the amount this time." Mr Kenneth Long, transport analyst at Kleinwort Grieveson said "It looks as if P&O is paying a fair price for a company going through a bit of a bad time."[2]

In the Port of Larne, one of the more noticeable results of the new arrangements was the change in the livery of the vessels to the familiar blue and white of P&O, with the distinctive Company flag. The story of the Port was now part of the world-wide history of the historic parent company which began life in 1835 as the Peninsular Steam Navigation Company. In the same way that the award of a mail contract from the Post Office had laid the foundation of the sea-link between Larne and Stranraer in the 19th century, the Peninsular Steam Navigation Company prospered because it was awarded the mail contract to Spain, Portugal and Gibraltar in 1837.

The Company serviced the Iberian Peninsula with seven paddle steamers, and as a result developed its distinctive quartered flag - the red and gold of the Spanish royal house of Aragon and Castile, and the blue and white of the Portuguese Braganzas. Most people today who notice the P&O flag in a wide range of settings, from ships on the high seas to large container lorries on motorways, would be unaware of its exotic origins. Following its success in Spain, Portugal and Gibraltar, the Company was awarded the monopoly on the Indian, Far Eastern and Australian mail runs, and expanded its formal title to the more familiar - The Peninsular and Oriental Steam Navigation Company - P&O for convenience.

The colourful history of this Company is worthy of a book in itself[3], and the vessels plying the routes to and from India and the Orient carried not only mail but also army personnel, young women in search of suitable husbands, all kinds of other entrepreneurs and adventurers, a multitude of ships officers and crews, tradesmen, labourers, and virtually anyone who had any reason - legitimate or otherwise - to be associated with the ships of the line. An unproven but romantic tradition also attributes to P&O a new term in the English language.

> "It was no wonder that when passengers booked their cabin in these ships,
> they stipulated 'port-outward, starboard-home', to obtain accommodation
> on the cool side of the ship as it steamed down the Red Sea and across the
> Arabian Sea in the days before air-conditioning. Nor was it any wonder the

acronym thus produced by the booking-clerk's abbreviation has come to mean privileged and swanky."[4]

In other words P-O-S-H.

By contrast, however, the prevailing weather at Larne rarely led to travellers taking precautions against the sun, and the paramount need to protect people from the robust Northern climate had been well-met by the new Passenger Terminal and walkway. Another major contribution to the improvement of the harbour facilities was the development of the old Mail Quay. In 1964 it had been modernised, but rather than build a completely new structure more than 20 years later, it was found to be more economical to utilise the existing piling, while lengthening and deepening the quay itself. Construction on the £3.5 million scheme, which included a two-deck ramp, was partly assisted by the European Regional Development Fund and Government Port Modernisation Grants. Over the years, the ERDF's major contribution to the development of modern facilities at the Port was greatly appreciated.

The quay was formally opened and re-named on 14 October 1987 by Mrs Patricia MacKean, widow of the former Chairman of Larne Harbour Ltd. The Board had proposed the name change to honour the MacKean family's long and distinguished association with the Company. The work of modernisation at the Port continued, and in 1993 the formal opening of the re-furbished Curran Quay was carried out by a young Scot with a reputation for leadership and skill on the sports field - Gavin Hastings, the captain of the British Lions Rugby team.

The development, mentioned earlier, of the high-tech Distribution Centre and the new one-stop Freight Check-in Centre on the Redlands Estate, enabled freight drivers to have their vehicles weighed, checked-in and marshalled in a single smooth and fast operation - again good examples of the Port identifying customers needs ahead of demand. The Distribution Centre was opened officially on 4 July 1996 by Baroness Denton of Wakefield, the then Northern Ireland Minister for the Economy, Agriculture and Womens' Issues. Reclamation work on the Harbour Estate continued, and the Port steadily developed the infrastructure for continued expansion to meet the increasing needs of new and established customers.

The Board was constantly aware, for many years, of the need for improvements in the quality of the road links on both sides of the Channel. This had some effect, though much remained to be done, but in May 1998 the Government announced a £10 million scheme to further improve the

Mrs Patricia MacKean, wife of a former Chairman, Major George MacKean, when she officially named the MacKean Quay – in honour of the family and to mark their service to the port. Presenting the bouquet is Margaret Magee, a member of staff in the Larne Harbour office.

Gavin Hastings, Captain of the British Lions Rugby Team pictured with (centre) Graeme Dunlop, Chairman of P&O European Ferries and Larne Harbour Ltd., and Denis Galway, Director and General Manager of Larne Harbour Ltd., at the official opening of the refurbished Curran Quay in 1993.

approach road to Larne. The work was scheduled for completion in 2002. The Port also played its part in the general improvement of local services, and the construction by Phoenix Gas of a £7 million gas pipeline across the Lough and through the Company's land gave local consumers a wider choice of energy sources.

By the beginning of the new Millennium, the Port of Larne was among the busiest on the Irish Sea, handling nearly 40 ferry arrivals and departures daily, around the clock. The RO/RO facilities dealt with a wide variety of shipping, including the most modern high-speed ferries, and Larne also had its facilities for a large range of bulk and general cargoes, including rock armour, stone aggregate, steel, fertiliser, and building and forest products. As well, the Port's three twin-level and one single-deck ramps could deal with large, heavy and abnormal loads in excess of 180 tonnes. In the autumn of 1998, the Port handled a massive load of 324 tonnes, which arrived at Larne on a special heavy-lift RO/RO vessel.

In the early Nineties, the Port received another commercial plaudit when Dr Tony O'Reilly, then Chairman, President and Chief Executive Officer of HJ Heinz and Company, told Northern Ireland businessmen at a meeting in Belfast that Larne had been a critical element in the decision to set up a Heinz frozen food plant in Ireland. England and Wales had also been considered for the 200-job project, but access to facilities at the Port made Ireland more attractive. Dr O'Reilly said "Larne represents a quite dynamic export port - it is economical, efficient and dedicated towards a high level of service." Not surprisingly this led to Larne running an advertisement titled "Larne Meanz Business". The Port also supported the Government job-creating agencies North and South-the Industrial Development Board in Northern Ireland, and the Industrial Development Authority in the Irish Republic - in their continual search for new inward investment. Significantly, the completion of the cross-Belfast rail link also meant that direct railway access to Larne became possible on an all-Ireland basis.

Though there was steady progress throughout the late Eighties and early Nineties, the Port suffered a setback in 1995 when Stena Sealink moved its operation to Belfast to establish a new route to Stranraer. Inevitably there was an initial downturn in business at Larne, but notwithstanding, the Port and its people rose to the challenge, and by the beginning of the new Millennium

Captain Val Plant, one of the Jetliner captains. 'It's the way forward on ferry travel'.

The Jetliner offered a new kind of service – with one of the Customer Services Managers, Rita Ratcliffe.

Photos: Alf McCreary

the number of tourist and commercial vehicles had increased steadily.

The decision by Stena to withdraw from Larne and to establish a new Belfast-Stranraer link, using conventional vessels and a new high-speed HSS ferry, had been the subject of speculation in the local media for some months. It was announced publicly in the autumn of 1995, and Stena claimed that the move would greatly improve their business.[5]

Whatever they thought in private, the management of Larne Harbour Ltd kept a tight upper-lip in public, apart from expressing regret at the Stena Sealink decision to which they claimed that they were permitted no input. The dispute went to law and after protracted discussions the case was settled out of court in the Spring of 1999, some four years after the initial announcement from Stena.

The immediate effect of the Stena withdrawal from Larne was a significant reduction in the number of vehicles passing through the Port. In 1995 this total was 832,176, and in 1996 the figure dropped to 488,346. The reduction in commercial vehicles was less dramatic - reducing from 375,077 in 1995, to 280,099 in 1996. The overall reduction was also due to a drop in tourist figures caused by poor

The Fleetwood Connection

The Larne to Fleetwood connection began on 25 April, 1973 when P&O Ferrymasters inaugurated a lift-on/ lift-off service (LO/LO). Two years later, on 23 February, 1975, a roll-on/roll-off (RO/RO) service was started on the same route by Pandoro Ltd, and the Fleetwood ferry became one of the mainstays of the Port of Larne.

It was particularly popular with hauliers who wanted direct access to North-West England, and especially to the motorways near Fleetwood and Liverpool. In the early days, Pandoro operated one ship daily to Fleetwood and another to Liverpool, but eventually concentrated on the former. As part of the service, the ships provided good cabin accommodation and a free hot and cold buffet.

The Captains on these vessels had a wide experience of tidal and weather conditions, and they exhibited not only considerable seamanship, but also great affection for their ships. Typical of these was Captain Martin Ingham, who was Master on a number of vessels including the European Navigator. He started his career at sea at 16 - following in the footsteps of his father and grandfather who had also been seamen. Martin began as a deck boy and later studied for his officer's qualifications. Like many another mariner he spent his early years on deep-sea vessels, and later served on cross-channel ferries. He said "When you are Master, you spend nearly 50 per cent of your time on the ship, and it becomes like your home. It is important to try to create a family atmosphere, and although there is a great deal of hard work involved, a life at sea has its own rewards".

The Larne-Fleetwood crossing, during more than a quarter-century of unbroken service, grew in popularity, and in 1999 P&O provided a third ship for the route, to meet the demand from hauliers and also an increasing number of motorists who wanted direct access to the Lancashire coast and the M6 motorway. Shortly into the Millennium, the RO/RO service celebrated its 25th anniversary, a testimony to its stability and progress through decades of change in the ferry business.

The European Pioneer, a regular on the long-established Larne – Fleetwood route.

Photo: Hal Mullin

FERRY COMPANY ENDS MONTHS OF SPECULATION

SEALINK PULLS PLUG ON LARNE

By MARCUS McCOLLUM and DIANE WHARRY

... But returns within five years!

summer weather and the Troubles in Northern Ireland. By the end of 1998, however, the overall figure had risen to 494,827. In January 1999, the Director and General Manager Denis Galway was able to tell members of the House of Commons Northern Ireland Affairs Committee on a visit to Larne that, in the previous year, the number of tourist vehicles had increased by 11.8 per cent, and commercial vehicles by 8.7 per cent, compared to 1997.

The Port, clearly, was fighting back, but like many other businesses in Northern Ireland, it suffered greatly from the continued political unrest, the resultant lack of tourists, and the continued extra costs of expensive security and other measures to comply with Government regulations. Larne did well in the circumstances, but under the more buoyant conditions of normality, as it is understood in the rest of the United Kingdom, there is no knowing what the Port could have achieved in the last 30 years or so of the 20th century. The same could be said of Northern Ireland itself.

What was noticeable, apart from the immediate effect on business of the withdrawal of Stena, was the determination with which everyone at the Port of Larne faced the new challenges. There was an added incentive to continue to prove that Larne was a major Irish port offering high-quality attractions, not only for smooth access and turnaround, but also for storage and other facilities. A similar positive and entrepreneurial spirit to that which had spurred on James Chaine, and later Colonel Frank Bustard, was evident.

The Pride of Rathlin, built at Rotterdam in 1972 and converted at Bremerhaven. A conventional ferry, she provided sterling service on the Larne–Cairnryan route.

Photo: P&O Ferries

"Jimmy Jetliner"

One of the best-known characters around the Port of Larne in the late 1990's was Jimmy Dowey, the Operations Superintendent. Part of his responsibility was to ensure that the loading operation on the Jetliner proceeded quickly and efficiently. With only 30 minutes for a complete turnaround , he and the loading officers on the vessel had no time to waste-particularly as it could carry up to 160 vehicles of different sizes, and a total of 600 passengers.

Jimmy, who joined P&O as a deckhand and rose quickly through the ranks to become a Chief Petty Officer, developed a keen eye for assessing the height, length and width of each vehicle and for sizing up its place in the veritable jig-saw of loading the Jetliner. He said " Though the dimensions of each vehicle are available on the computer, you also have to develop that special knack of knowing where each vehicle will fit in, because you haven't time to go around measuring each one individually. In the end it all fits together, so that we can turn the Jetliner round quickly to meet her schedule, and to provide the best service possible for our customers."

Customer-service rated highly on Jimmy's list of priorities. "It can take a lot of money to attract people through advertising, so it is important to look after the customer. I go by the principle that if you treat people well, and really try to look after them, they will stay with you. It is important to make the extra effort. My job involves meeting all kinds of people, and working in all weathers, but I really love it."

In return, many of the regular travellers greeted Jimmy on the quayside like an old friend , and he became known affectionately as "Jimmy Jetliner", a nick-name which he took as a compliment.

Jimmy Dowey, P&O European Ferries Operations Superintendent at Larne. "It's important to look after the customer."

Picture courtesy of Omni Publications

The European Endeavour which joined the Larne-Cairnryan Service in 1995 to cater for increased freight demand.

Denis Galway said "The loss of Stena was undoubtedly a setback, but we faced this challenge and set out to attract new business. The welcome relocation of Stena Line to Larne from Autumn 2000 reaffirms and consolidates our position as Ireland's Premier RORO and Ferry Port. The first regular Larne to Stranraer service was established in 1872 and operated continuously until 1995 – it is good to see it back."

"Larne Harbour Limited and P&O have demonstrated their confidence in the future with the ongoing developments in Larne and also P&O's commitment on both sides of the Irish Sea. This includes the recently-opened Terminal at Cairnryan and new ships for the route, the Superstar Express and the European Causeway."

Towards the end of the decade there were encouraging increases in commercial and tourist vehicles passing through the Port. The Larne-Cairnryan ferries carried the bulk of the traffic, but there was a significant increase in business on the other routes. In 1999 P&O added a third vessel to the Fleetwood crossing (see page 185), and in the same year the demand was such for the Ardrossan service, re-established in 1992, that P&O were putting on extra sailings. Denis Galway said "This growth has been most heartening, and I am confident that Larne will continue to do well. Our success has been due in no small part to the hard work and skills of our employees at all levels, and we are most appreciative of their commitment to the continued prosperity of the Port".

The determination of Larne to compete strenuously for business was underlined by the provision of facilities for a fast ferry. P&O introduced the new Jetliner, which started service between Larne and Cairnryan on 12 June 1996, thus opening another important chapter in the history of the crossing. With four reversible water-jets capable of pushing through 44 tons of water per second, the vessel had a top operating speed of 32 knots. The fact that it could accelerate quickly out of the deep waters at Larne and Cairnryan, gave it a head-start against other rivals in completing the crossing in an hour.

Val Plant, one of the Captains on the Jetliner, helped in 1996 to bring the vessel from the shipyard in Bergen where it had been built. He was typical of the new breed of sailors on the Larne-Cairnryan route. Val went to sea at the age of 17 and spent 11 years in the Far East trade. After a brief spell on conventional ferries, he became a Second Officer with P&O Cruises and travelled all over the world, particularly to the Caribbean, Alaska and the South Seas.

He left deep-sea voyaging and returned to conventional and high-speed ferries travelling between Northern Ireland and Scotland. He said "I always wanted to go to sea and after travelling the world, I did what many other people do - I took a job on the ferries, which not only enabled me to put my training into practice but also gave me the opportunity to have a shore-based home. The Fast-ferries are an exciting way to sail. It's the way forward in ferry travel, and it is good to be in at the start. It is important to keep in touch regularly with the passengers on the crossings. We make them feel welcome on board and we keep them informed of developments en route."

The main conventional vessel on the Larne-Cairnryan run, up to the turn of the century, was the Pride of Rathlin. Built at Rotterdam in 1972, and converted at Bremerhaven in 1985-86, the Rathlin - previously known as Free Enterprise VII and Pride of Walmer - was a vessel of character. Like her sister ship Pride of Ailsa, which was sold in 1996, she was a familiar sight as she plied between Larne and Cairnryan in all weathers. She was also popular with those passengers who preferred conventional ferries, with her crews expressing a tremendous pride in her performance and service. She was well-named "Pride of Rathlin".

Captain Eddie Irvine, one of the Masters on the Rathlin, spent 10 years on deep-sea voyages and 30 on the ferries. He said "I was reared at Islandmagee and as a toddler I watched the boats coming

Captain Eddie Irvine, one of the masters on the Pride of Rathlin, spent 10 years on deep-sea voyages and 30 on the ferries. 'I never had any other ambition but to go to sea'.

A harpoon head recovered from Grytviken South Georgia by HMS Antrim, April 1982. The Commander of the vessel, which took part in the Falklands Campaign, presented it to Larne Harbour Ltd during a courtesy visit to the Port

Photos: Alf McCreary

in and out of Larne day and night. I never had any other ambition but to go to sea." He talked with affection about his ship. "She is a great seafaring vessel and you would be surprised at how many people prefer the older type of ship. The night sailings are the busiest, and the 4 am from Cairnryan is most popular with the hauliers who want to be in Northern Ireland by the next morning. Despite the challenges, there is great satisfaction in this job. And once you have berthed you feel that you have earned your wages."

Such sentiments are not new. They have been echoed down the ages by countless other seafarers who have sailed into and out of Larne. From the earliest times the Port has been a haven, and sometimes a target, for all types of craft from the Viking raiders and enemy vessels in times of pillage and violence, to a base for Allied shipping in wartime. It has been a welcome home for those who have returned to their native land, and a sad farewell for many who emigrated to foreign shores, never to return.

It has known times of tragedy when lives were lost, not least on the Princess Victoria, and it has also known periods of peace and prosperity. It has become a busy Port which has grown from a small harbour to a large modern complex offering the latest facilities for a wide variety of shipping, including some of the world's most technologically-advanced vessels.

Down the ages, many people have shown determination, courage and ingenuity in making Larne what it is today. They overcame early competition from rivals, they developed railways, they brought in the most advanced ships of the day, they survived World Wars and seafaring and commercial setbacks, they rose to the demands of constantly-changing commercial and tourist traffic, and they developed a Port which is well-placed to meet the challenges of the new Millennium.

They did so with style, and not a little native wit and humour. They included ordinary people who did their day's work and made their own mark, and many characters and well-known figures whose contribution was immense. As this volume on the history of the Port of Larne draws to a close at the beginning not only of a new century but of a new Millennium, it

Senior naval staff and directors and senior management of Larne Harbour Ltd during the visit of HMS Antrim to the Port.

is perhaps fitting to look back to James Chaine, that remarkable man whose vision and entrepreneurial skill set the Port of Larne on its way to prosperity so long ago.

The Chaine Tower is not only a memorial to him but to all others - including the late Colonel Frank Bustard - who put the Port of Larne on the map and have kept it there, with vision and determination. Perhaps the most fitting praise of all is the inscription on the Chaine Tower, borrowed from the commemoration to Sir Christopher Wren in St Paul's cathedral: "Si monumentum requiris circumspice"- "If you seek a monument, look around."

The bustle, size and vibrancy of the Port of Larne today is the best possible tribute to James Chaine and all the others whose vision of a thriving, successful port has been more than fulfilled. Given its history, and the skill, hard work, and determination of its people, the success story of this vintage yet truly modern Port looks set to continue well into the new Millennium and beyond.

The Chairman of Larne Harbour Ltd. Graeme Dunlop, third left, presenting a casting of a mooring bollard to Board Member Darwin Templeton to mark his long association with the Company. Also pictured are Board Members Denis Galway, extreme left, and Frank Ledwidge. Inset, is Board Member John Kearsley, Managing Director of P&O European Ferries (Irish Sea) Ltd.

Photo: Ivan Morrow

1. Lloyd's List 24 December 1985.
2. London Times, 5 December 1986.
3. "The Story of P&O" written by David Howarth and Stephen Howarth and published by Weidenfeld and Nicolson, London 1986 (revised edition 1994) gives a definitive account of the Company's history.
4. Richard Woodman "The History of the Ship" published by Conway Maritime Press 1997, p257.
5. Irish Independent, 6 September 1995, and other media outlets.

I N D E X